HAUNTED
IPSWICH

HAUNTED
IPSWICH

Pete Jennings

The History Press

Dedicated to Gippe – whoever he was.

First published 2010

The History Press
The Mill, Brimscombe Port
Stroud, Gloucestershire, GL5 2QG
www.thehistorypress.co.uk

British Library Cataloguing in Publication Data.
A catalogue record for this book is available from the British Library.

ISBN 978 0 7524 5660 7
Typesetting and origination by The History Press
Printed in Great Britain
Manufacturing managed by Jellyfish Print Solutions Ltd

CONTENTS

INTRODUCTION

Welcome to a collection of stories about my home town of Ipswich in Suffolk. I was born there in 1953, and have collected local ghost stories for over forty years. I have presented them to guests on Original Gemini Ghost Tours since 1996, together with my friend and colleague Ed Nicholls. People have been very kind in increasing our hoard of tales (as well as expanding upon the ones we already had the bare bones of), so thank you to everyone who has ever shared a story with me. Some stories start as a single sentence, such as 'they reckon there is something haunting that place...' Sometimes that is all I ever get to hear, and no further details are forthcoming, but often, when I offer to listen without prejudice, and research without jumping to conclusions, I discover more about this peculiar facet of local history. Researching ghost stories has led me to appreciate the complexity and diversity of Ipswich's rich history, and this in turn provides a solid context for what are often fleeting experiences. We certainly have no need to make up stories for our ghost tours – there are too many already to fit in, even after splitting the town centre into two routes.

There is no doubt that historically Ipswich has always been an important place. A Roman villa was established at Castle Hill. (Children once claimed to have seen a ghost of a Roman soldier at the nearby Dales parkland.) A Roman ford crossed the river Orwell, now spanned by the impressive Orwell Bridge, built in 1982; it is actually Britain's longest pre-stressed concrete bridge. (Those searching for ghoulish facts may note that the bridge had twenty suicides in its first two decades, the river claiming one sacrifice for each year.)

Ipswich was once a popular centre of pilgrimage, with the likes of Henry VIII, Catherine of Aragon and Anne Boleyn visiting the Chapel of Our Lady of Grace in the sixteenth century. One wooden statue was removed in the Reformation and sent to London to be burnt, but somehow got rescued by sailors and ended up in Nettuno, Italy, where it remains today. A replica was made in 2000 and placed in the medieval St Mary at the Elms Church (the nearest to the original Lady Lane site, which is marked with a plaque). At the rear of that Church is believed to be Ipswich's oldest inhabited house, The Cottage, dating to 1487.

As the maritime gateway to East Anglia, it was its importance as an Anglo-Saxon port that really established Ipswich in around AD 600. The Frisians who migrated into the area started making Ipswich Ware pottery, which is found across the UK in huge quantities from around AD 625-800. Later, Vikings thought it wealthy enough to make a major raid on it before the Battle of Maldon in 991. They defeated Ulfkytel, the Govenor of the East Angles, at Rushmere Heath, and the Danes ruled East Anglia for a long period. Later, in 1010, an army of Danes led by Anlaf marched through the town *en route* to the Battle of Ringsmere near Thetford.

The Normans built a castle on The Mount, where the modern police station stands in Elm Street, and the nearby St Mary at Elms Church has a Norman arched doorway. They would have wanted to impress their authority on the town: Earl Gyrth had led a large war band of Saxons at the Battle of Hastings in 1066, and was killed on the battlefield alongside 80 per cent of the Ipswich Burgesses.

The Puritans of the Eastern Association had a stronghold here in the English Civil War. Royal Naval ships were built, provisioned and repaired in Ipswich from the sixteenth to nineteenth centuries. Pilgrims set sail in several ships from the port to America, and the Port of Ipswich continues to be an important centre of commerce. Remarkably, the town has a total of fourteen parks, so one is never far from some green space.

Uniquely for such a historic town, Museum Street has not got a museum! It moved to High Street and has some excellent collections, complemented by another museum and gallery at Christchurch Mansion. The original 1847 custom-built museum is now known as Arlingtons. In the days before its collections outgrew the available space it saw free lectures given by Charles Darwin's tutor John Henslow.

The town, with a population of around 128,000, gave the world Ransomes' agricultural equipment and Fisons' fertilizers, and has also gone on to be national headquarters for Willis Corroon and Guardian Royal Insurances as well as BT Telecommunications.

Ipswich has produced sporting heroes, including Alf Ramsey and Bobby Robson, two of the former 'Tractor Boy' Ipswich Town FC managers who went on to manage England. Ipswich has had a professional football club since 1936; the team replaced the amateur Ipswich Association of Football, founded in 1878. Rugby player Prince Alexander Obolensky scored the two tries that enabled England to beat the All Blacks for the first time; Karen Pickering, the Olympic swimmer, and the successful Ipswich Witches speedway team are other notable local sportsmen.

I am proud to show folk around the nooks and crannies of Ipswich, but will happily admit that most towns have a similar wealth of material if only someone takes the time to listen, research and explore. Certainly I do not believe every ghost story I hear. Some are genuinely mistaken interpretations of natural events, others the result of too much alcohol, whilst there will also be the odd individual making up tales deliberately. However, even if one discounts 90 per cent of all the tales one encounters, there still remains that 10 per cent that intrigues and stimulates the mind to wonder 'what if?' Many of my sources wish to remain anonymous because they believe they will be open to ridicule. I don't blame them and respect their choice, especially since some have responsible positions – including policemen, doctors and teachers.

I do not believe it is my job to convince people whether ghosts exist or not. I just present the stories and let people make their own mind up. Having said that, I freely admit that I believe in the supernatural, and I am consequently a biased observer! I also believe that everyone has some psychic ability, but it is an ability that is better developed in some people than others, just like any other talent. We are often forced to conform to other people's ideas of 'normal' behaviour, and I think that many people suppress their gift because they are frightened of it, are cautious of being labelled a loony or have simply been conditioned as a child 'not to tell lies and fancy stories.' Consequently, children and animals, who have not been conditioned by society, are often good indicators of genuine psychic activity – they simply react honestly to what they observe or feel.

Whether you are a resident of Ipswich or a far-flung armchair traveller, I hope you enjoy and are stimulated by what I present here. As you will find, my own interest stems from a tale my mother told me in my early teens. Since then, I have only ever seen one ghost – and that was not in Ipswich, and was after nearly forty years of fruitless exploration. My interest in the supernatural runs parallel to a fascination for history, and this is often crucial for understanding the phenomena in context.

There is one form of story that I have deliberately not included: secret tunnels. I feel that there has been more than enough rot written and speculation made about the existence of such features. Some are just large extended cellars or sewers. It wasn't uncommon for the cellar of one building to connect to another. The same happens with the loft spaces in the roofs of terraced houses – I know, because I was once burgled via one in Cemetery Road, Ipswich (an appropriate ex-address for anyone interested in ghosts). Most old buildings (including several in Ipswich) have tunnel stories attached to them. They are frequently credited with running for miles underground between significant old buildings. What you have to consider is how they would be constructed without anyone finding out about them at the time. A tunnel that is not secret seems rather pointless for fleeing enemies or making romantic trysts. Removing soil from secret tunnels was a problem for prisoners of war trying to escape during the Second World War, men who were only attempting modest efforts. Even if the engineering ability existed to construct lengthy holes beneath the ground (doubtful before Victorian expertise and technology was available) disposing of the spoil heaps without arousing suspicion would have been a monumental task. Whilst I will agree that some old buildings may have short secret exit tunnels, I think that anything longer would be quite rare unless you were excavating from existing caves (such as the Hellfire Caves in the Chiltern Hills of Buckinghamshire). Our lack of surface rock in Suffolk (and surfeit of soft sand and clay around Ipswich) would preclude any such ambitious structures without a vast quantity of shoring up and pit props.

In writing this book, I have tried to put the sequence of stories and sites in an order that can be walked either in one day or in several sections, suggested by the chapter headings. Having said that, there are one or two sites far from the town centre that do not fit easily into any compact route, so I have included them at the end of chapter one.

Who knows what a ghost is? The only true authorities are the ghosts themselves – and they are not telling. It is notable, however, that most of the world's varied religions do talk of an afterlife of some description. From a scientific basis, nothing is ever destroyed: it is merely changed in form, so our rotting bodies feed plants, which in turn feed animals, which often feed us, I guess. We are also creatures of energy, and we are taught it also cannot be destroyed, so what happens to the electricity that powers our brain and nervous system? What form it takes after death is an interesting question that as yet seems not to have a set of satisfactory answers.

If we make efforts in life to create things, they will often live on after our deaths, and form part of our ongoing reputation. Our forebears placed great importance on reputation, since if people still spoke of you after you had gone it was a form of immortality.

There are theories about earthbound spirits of the dead unable to move on until they have accepted their death or passed on a message. There are also theories of walls being imprinted with 'recordings' of vivid memories and replaying them like a video recorder. I do not know whether any or all of these theories are true, but hope that the stories here may help you to come to some decision about your own personal beliefs.

Pete Jennings, 2010

one

FAMILY STORIES

Some Family Stories

If it wasn't for my mother I may never have got involved with ghost stories. She was a very down-to-earth person, embarrassed to be thought of as any different from anyone else, and yet she admitted to me, when I was about twelve or thirteen years old, that she had twice seen a ghost. If it had been my father I should have thought it a 'tall tale', but because my mother was such a straightforward sort of person, with a suspicion of anything fanciful, I had to believe her.

Phyllis Howe (as she was called when single) worked in service in the 1930s. Before marrying my father, Ron Jennings, she worked for the Zagni family of Ipswich. Now many people know the Zagni family because of their business (they created the excellent Peter's Ice Cream), but my mother worked as live-in cook for a different branch of that Italian family. They owned the Zagni Asphalt Co., and had a house in Hutland Road, Ipswich, named after an area of military huts connected to nearby barracks. The company were at 73-9 Hutland Road until 2003. You can still see the old Zagni Yard at No. 79 on the corner. My mother replaced another cook who left to get married (as she was to do herself in turn). There was also a daily maid, the master and mistress and their daughter Bonnie, who was in her early twenties.

My mother described how, one day, she had walked from the garden and entered the kitchen, which was long and narrow. To her surprise she saw a man sitting on a chair halfway up the kitchen. He was reading a newspaper, which obscured his face, but she noticed that he had his feet drawn up to the seat of the chair. It was the custom not to idly enter a kitchen in such households: not only was it a courtesy to the cook, who needed to get on with her work, but also for safety, with open cooking ranges and boiling saucepans about. Phyllis did not mind too much and wondered if it was a young man waiting for Bonnie – though, despite being an attractive young woman, suitors did not usually call for her. She carried on up the kitchen, but as she approached the man she felt that something was not 'quite right'. To her dismay, the figure faded and then vanished as she drew level! Screaming, she ran into the main part of the house.

Hutland Road – the old Zagni Asphalt site.

Mrs Zagni quickly appeared, sat her down and offered a drink of water. When Phyllis recovered, she described what she had seen. Mrs Zagni did not seem too surprised. 'It sounds like my late son-in-law,' she declared. 'I did not know you had one,' replied Phyllis. Mrs Zagni then went on to explain that when Bonnie was young she had a good friend who was a boy. They said that they would get married when they got older, and, unlike so many other childhood sweethearts, they actually did. Unfortunately, in his teens Bonnie's husband caught tuberculosis – a killer disease in those days. He was unable to take on a job to support his wife-to-be, but her parents said that the couple could live with them. They even had a small garden house built for him, since lots of fresh air was recommended for such cases. In the summer he often slept in it to avoid keeping the family awake with his coughing in the night. In the morning he would come back into the house and fetch the master's discarded newspaper from the breakfast table. To keep out of the way of the clearing up he often sat in the kitchen, typically with a habit of curling up his feet onto the chair. Sadly, the young man had eventually succumbed to the disease; his picture had been put in a drawer, and the garden house was dismantled so as not to serve as a constant reminder to Bonnie.

Mrs Zagni showed a picture of him to mother, but as she had not seen the apparition's face she could not say for sure that it was him. 'You must have the second sight, my dear,' comforted Mrs Zagni, adding, 'On your day off we sometimes hold a séance here.' (The Spiritualist movement and clairvoyants were very popular at the time.) 'Maybe you would like to join us?'

'Not blooming likely!' mother replied, and never saw the ghost again. She left and got married, first living in Rosemary Lane, but later moving to 261 Landseer Road at the start of the Second World War. It was a new council house built on old farmland. She confided in me that not long after she moved in she saw what she thought might be a farmer, gazing across the living room. A few weeks later she saw him again, and summoned the courage to speak, asking him who he was and if she could she help him. He disappeared and was not seen again. She said she wondered if it was the old farmer come to see what had happened to his land. I was born in that house in 1953, but never saw anything during my time there. I did, however, acquire a life-long interest in ghost stories, which eventually lead me to write and lecture about them, as well as creating Original Gemini Ghost Tours of Ipswich with my friend Ed Nicholls, a group which has been running since 1997.

The Ghosts of Kemble Street and Other Suburbs

Ed has his own family story, which has as its basis a house at 23 Kemble Street, where his grandparents used to live until 1978. Someone on one of our tours mentioned that they lived in that very same house, and sometimes heard loud snoring from next door, despite it being vacant. Ed was able to tell them that in his grandparents' time they had commented upon the loud snoring that they could hear through the thin dividing wall. It came from their next-door neighbour, Mr Barnes, but he had long since died!

Just as Kemble Street is away from the town centre off Foxhall Road, there are other locations away from the town centre with less well-known hauntings. In the 1940s there were frequent sightings of a lady photographer ghost at Rose Hill School's assembly hall. Another haunted school was exposed by a policeman parked up to do some paperwork in 1976. He saw a man in an overcoat emerge from Chantry High School. Suspecting he was a burglar, the policeman left his car to apprehend him – but

No. 23 Kemble Street,
home of a ghostly snorer.

the 'burglar' faded in front of his eyes. Unwisely, he wrote it up in his pocket book, much to the amusement of his colleagues back at the police station.

A house in Bulwer Road has heavy-footed phantoms stomping around upstairs. Maybe it is James Redford Bulwer QC, the MP for Ipswich 1874-80 after whom the road is named?

In nearby London Road one of the elevated town houses at the town end is subject to occasional haunting by a vague misty figure. Staff who worked at the old Anglesea Road hospital had an apparition in their old operating theatre, and at St Clement's Hospital the ghastly spirit of a female suicide holds her bleeding arms before her as she slowly moves along a corridor near to a bathroom.

Awful Orford Street

I experienced something myself in Orford Street once, although I have to admit I did not actually see a ghost. I was looking for a house to live in, close to the town centre and in a good state of repair (since I am not the best DIY handyman). It also had to be within a modest budget limit. From the masses of inappropriate details I was sent by various estate agents, one stood out as 'ticking all the boxes'. The house was vacant, so the agent agreed to pick me up in his car and show me around himself. From the outside it looked perfect.

The front door led straight into the reception room, which was tastefully decorated. After standing in it for a minute or two, I suddenly felt an overwhelming sensation of dread. I did not even go through to the kitchen area or upstairs, but asked to leave straight away. Outside in the car I apologised to the agent for wasting his time, but did not give the reason. I did not need to. He told me I was the third person he

Gippeswyk Hall.

had taken there who had reacted in such a way. 'The last one did get as far as the kitchen,' he nervously laughed. He offered to show me some other places, and in fact I bought one of them. I can reflect that despite age, appearance or even a bargain price, some buildings have a definite atmosphere that can be shared by many without prior knowledge. A friend who lives in that area later told me that the house, despite its good position, frequently changes hands.

Supplementary Spectres

In the 1960s a ghost of a small child in a nightdress was reported in a Waterford Road house, together with the sound of footsteps upstairs, and a mysterious mist. The occupants were so scared that they moved out at very short notice. That is not the only child ghost we will encounter. I always think it much more tragic when a child dies, their future cut short, but the ghost of a blonde young boy reported at a house in Felixstowe Road in 1989 had a smile on his face.

A lady in the late 1990s saw the ghost of a slim old man in a suit on her stairs at Skylark Lane on the Chantry Estate. Gyppeswyck Hall near Gyppeswyck Avenue is haunted at the full moon by a ghostly white lady upstairs. One person also commented on seeing mist emerging from the chimney, despite knowing no fires were lit. The building is now occupied by a training company.

Many of the stories you will find in this book have been supplied by members of the public, via our tours, my old radio show or the local paper. Sometimes they have been pieced together as fragments over several years, as you shall find in this next case...

two

THE BUTTERMARKET AREA

Bewilderment at the Buttermarket

Although built as a modern shopping centre in 1990, the Buttermarket is sited over some ancient ruins of Ipswich. A large Anglo-Saxon graveyard and a Carmelite White Priory founded around 1278 lay beneath its foundations. A row of medieval houses stood where the columns are situated on St Stephen's Lane (opposite the old Sun Inn, now a shop). One house was found to have burnt down (from evidence of melted glass and metal) and the remains of a frail basket were located in the cellar. Contained within were half a dozen charcoal, oval shapes. Laboratory analysis revealed them to be the remains (or the ghosts) of some sour dough rolls turned to charcoal by the heat of the fire, the only medieval cooking to survive in England. A museum worker tried to recreate them from a recipe derived from the laboratory results. We were disappointed to find that although traditional ingredients had been used (unpasteurised milk, sea salt and untreated flour) the rolls turned out rock hard and tasted awful!

Under the Ground

Beneath the shopping complex is an underground car park. One night in 2007, when the car park and shops had closed, the lady in charge left her office to empty a coin machine. She returned quickly to the office without emptying it, though, when she sensed movement. Anxiously she rang her boss, who came over within ten minutes. She let him into the premises and they looked around, but no source of movement could be found. Locking up, he said he would ask to see the CCTV footage the next morning. Imagine their horror at seeing the shadows on the wall either side of the machine moving with frenetic activity on the time-coded video! The boss said he did not know what to think. There were no windows, trees or moving lamps down there, or anything else to explain the phenomenon. Deciding on practicality, he announced that he thought it poor working practice to have a lone worker in such a situation to handle cash, and would ensure a second member of staff would be on hand in future.

*St Stephen's Church and
the Buttermarket Centre.*

The Secrets of the Ancient House

The Ancient House is probably the best known and most beautiful old building in
Ipswich. It stands on the corner of the Buttermarket thoroughfare and St Stephen's
Lane. It was built in the mid-1500s, and soon became the property of the Sparrowe
family, who passed it down for many generations. When I was young it was a popular
independent bookshop, and I would pester my mother to take me there, not just
to satisfy my passion for books, but to visit the 'secret' priest hole that had been
discovered. They charged an old sixpence to enter, and there was a wax effigy of
Charles II sitting on a chair within. It was believed at the time that he had hidden
there after fleeing defeat from the Battle of Worcester in 1651, but we now know that
this is incorrect – he left England from the South Coast. (Ipswich would have been a
poor choice – it had ships, but was also strongly Puritan.) The room may have hidden
other Cavalier fugitives, but was most likely used to conceal Catholic priests travelling
in secret to celebrate Mass with those clinging to the Roman Catholic faith. Certainly
the Sparrowe family were, unusually for Ipswich, of the Royalist persuasion, and they
were kept under house arrest for much of the English Civil Wars. I remember also an
enormous wall painting of John the Baptist on the stairs. Hidden in the private rooms
was a picture of one of the ancestors who, family legend stated, had been eaten alive

The Ancient House – the haunt of Widow Lakland?

by rats, although no one remembered how it had happened. Curiously enough, he was called Gosnall and had been involved in the persecution and execution of nine Protestant martyrs in the 1500s – but more of that later. Many of the family are buried in the crypt of nearby St Lawrence's Church in Dial Lane.

In the late 1960s I had a girlfriend with a Saturday job at the shop, and I sometimes met her when she finished work. Once she told me how the older staff had been trying to frighten her with stories of a Grey Lady ghost. She laughed dismissively and said that she had never experienced anything, and I thought no more of it at the time; over the years, however, I heard more reports of the Grey Lady ghost dressed in a wide flowing dress.

The bookshop closed down, and eventually the lease was taken on by Lakeland Plastics, later to become Lakeland Ltd. They already had a chain of shops, and moved one of their employees from another town to become the new manager. He recruited local staff and prepared to open the store in a run up to Christmas. Inevitably he was told about the ghost by the locals, but thought it a bit of a tease for him, the incomer. A couple of displays fell over for no apparent reason, and this was blamed on the ghost. One night, after the rest of the staff had gone home, the manager worked on late to finish a display. Like many of us, he misplaced his scissors. He was startled to find them in the next room, despite being sure he had not gone in there. Determined to get to the bottom of the matter, he contacted a Spiritualist medium from his old town, and asked her to visit. By the time this was arranged, the shop had been open for a few days; it was just before Christmas 1997.

She met him straight away, and assured him that there was a female presence there from long ago. She asked if she could wander about whilst he got on with running the store to see what else she could find out. (She was a stranger to the town and said that she did not know the history of the place.) A while later, she returned to him and confirmed the presence of the apparition. She added that the woman seemed upset. She had tried to obtain her name, but all that went through her head was the Lakeland name prominently displayed around the building. On leaving, the manager reflected that she seemed genuine, and that maybe the locals were not having a joke at his expense after all…

I was told about this development one morning. Coincidentally, I was visiting Suffolk County Archives that afternoon on a very different quest: to find out what Matthew Hopkins, the self-styled 'Witchfinder General', had got up to in Ipswich. He was a son of the vicar of Great Wenham, just outside Ipswich, and worked in the town for a shipping company practising maritime law. Some books say that he was a lawyer, but there is no evidence that he ever qualified; it seems he was poorly thought of locally, and ended up returning to live in Mistley, near Manningtree, just over the Essex border. Then, after 'exposing' three witches in his home parish, he came up with a lucrative plan: styling himself 'the Witchfinder General', he went from town to town offering to get rid of witches – for a price. His bill was usually steep: a bill of £23, for example, was paid by Stowmarket council, a fortune at that time. He was assisted by two companions, John Stearne and Mary Phillips (who searched females for him), plus an army of paid informers, who tipped him off as to who was unpopular in any place he planned to visit.

His travels, which took place around 1644-5, took him from Essex, through Suffolk and Norfolk and on to Cambridgeshire and Huntingdonshire. Suspects were kept awake for days on end and continually questioned; they were made to stand or walk for this period without being allowed to rest. They were pricked with a pin, and if they did not react each time were labelled as having 'the Devil's mark', an insensitive piece of flesh believed to be 'a teat' to feed their familiars. Some were 'swum' in ponds with their thumbs tied to their toes; some drowned before their guilt or innocence was judged. Many confessed to end their torment, and were hanged, the usual penalty for witches under English law. Scotland and the Continent usually burnt them at the stake. Many of the confessions seem remarkably similar, but they are quite incredible in places.

It is estimated that Hopkins was responsible for the deaths of about 400 people in East Anglia, about 10 per cent of that figure being male. Many of them were poor widows dependent on Parish Relief, and thus disliked by neighbours who had to meet the cost of keeping them. It is doubtful whether many – or indeed any – were genuine witches, and it is likely that prejudice was a contributing factor to their fate, and that they were scapegoats for any mishaps in their villages. For example, a poor woman might ask for alms, and mutter to herself if she was sent away empty handed. This could be interpreted as 'cursing', particularly if someone then fell ill or a hen stopped laying eggs.

Even people found not guilty probably had their lives ruined; many would have lost friends, jobs and lodgings through acquiring 'bad reputations'. Hopkins was able to flourish and amass a fortune in the fourteen months he was active. Some people have wondered why he was accepted so easily – was everybody so superstitious, so credulous? Certainly some were, and others went along with the mob mentality fearing for their own safety if they did not. Chaos was rife at the time, as friends and family members fought each other; Britain was filled with 'doom mongers' declaring that the end of the world was nigh.

However, there is a frequently ignored factor: the use of Hopkins by the Roundhead cause. It is known that at least three times top commanders met with him. Why should they want to meet a failed shipping clerk if he was of no use to them? The inference is that he was instructed to include some suspected Royalist sympathisers or spies in his witch hunts, and get rid of them. After all, minimal proof was required to convict a witch. In exchange he could operate as he pleased without their interference. He also employed a network of spies and informers, invaluable for use in military campaigns against people whose loyalties were uncertain. Eventually he was denounced from the pulpit (and via a pamphlet) as a charlatan by John Guale, the vicar of Staughton in Huntingdonshire, and lost influence. As John wrote in 1646, 'Every old woman with a wrinkled face, a furrowed brow, a hairy lip, a gobber tooth, a squint eye, a squeaking voice or scolding tongue, having a rugged coat on her back, a skull-cap on her head, a spindle in her hand and a dog or cat by her side, is not only suspect but pronounced for a witch.'

Hopkins was thrown into a pond by some disgruntled villagers, and disappeared from the records soon after that. Some have speculated that he went to New England like his brother Thomas, or to Salem in America (famous for its own witch trials of 1692, after his death) or even that he was convicted of witchcraft himself in Suffolk. The truth, discovered recently, is less dramatic: apparently he died of consumption (nowadays known as tuberculosis). He was buried in St Mary's Churchyard, Mistley, on 12 August 1647. It no longer has a Church on site, but the graveyard can be seen. My visit to the archives produced some names of people arrested on Hopkins' evidence in Ipswich. The records of the Ipswich Borough Sessions show that six people were charged at that time, including a married couple, James and Mary Emerson. They were accused of sending lice to Mary and Robert Ward by witchcraft. They were sent to trial at Bury St Edmunds and sentenced to a year's imprisonment and to be stood in the pillory four times. James was found not guilty of the greater charge of murdering Richard Greye, and his wife was found not guilty of sending lice to John Seeley.

However, another victim, Alice Denham, was found guilty of felony, witchcraft and feeding imps. She was hanged, yet Rose Parker (the wife of Christopher) was found not guilty of 'murdering John Cole, witchcraft, felony and feeding imps'. Margaret Sutton (the wife of James) was made to pay sureties for her future good behaviour after being charged with felony and witchcraft.

All of the accused mentioned above were charged in Ipswich around the same time, but sent for trial at Bury St Edmunds. Notice that only one person was condemned to

Matthew Hopkins, 'the Witchfinder General'.

death and another got off with no penalty at all, showing that it was not inevitable that someone accused of witchcraft would be found guilty and hanged. (Also note that the five included one man.) It is likely that many people got sent out of their own area for trial at the time. With the Civil Wars raging and locals away fighting (or under arrest), many courts were closed. However, the final of the six Ipswich residents accused by Hopkins stood trial in Ipswich: Widow Mary Lakland.

Having heard the story about Lakeland Plastics in the morning, her name stood out. She was accused of many criminal acts: killing her husband John, murdering Elisabeth Aldham and Sarah Clarke (the servant of my namesake, Mrs Jennings), 'wasting away' the body of John Beales, and burning the ship of Henry Reade – as well as the more usual 'nourishing of sprites', in her case allegedly two dogs and a mole. John Beales, the man whose body Lakland allegedly caused to wither, was the private tutor to Mary's grandchild – evidence that her family had money. Mary was not the usual 'poor widow' suspect. In fact, it was alleged at her trial that, after killing her husband, she attacked John Beales 'because he would not have her.' In other words, he rejected her advances (perhaps fearing he would meet the same fate as her recently departed husband?).

Just as today, trial records detailed the age, profession and address of the victims. In the case of Mary Lakland's husband, this is highly illuminating: he was 'a barber who doth dwell above his business in St Stephen's Lane.' A barber in those days was a good middle-class profession, since most acted as surgeons as well (and were often rated better than doctors). Therefore it was not surprising that there was money for a private tutor. More compelling evidence, though, is the address: the Ancient House lies on the corner of the Buttermarket and St Stephen's Lane, so the Laklands were near neighbours of the Sparrowe family at the Ancient House. Were they friends? We do not know, but the Sparrowe family, under house arrest, would have relied upon neighbours to bring their supplies. It could easily have led to one of them being suspected as a Royalist sympathiser, spy or informer. Although I cannot prove it, Widow Mary Lakland – whose eye for a gentleman so soon after losing her husband was bound to make her puritanical neighbours disapprove – may well have fallen victim to Hopkins and the mob because of her friendship with the Sparrowes. Why was she not sent for trial with the rest to Bury St Edmunds? As we have already seen, being sent for trial was not a guaranteed outcome; however, if she was put on trial locally one could rely upon a solidly Puritan jury to convict her. Mary Lakland was found guilty of many of her alleged crimes and burnt at the stake on 9 September 1645.

Did I not say earlier that the penalty for witchcraft in England was hanging? The answer to the mystery lies within arcane seventeenth-century law, and some of the hypocrites that operated it. Mary had been found guilty of killing her husband, who at that time was considered legally to be the representative of the king in each household. If you killed the king it was treason. Therefore if you killed the representative of the king, it was petty treason, for which the penalty was being burnt at the stake – this despite the fact that the Puritans who convicted her had supported the execution of King Charles I, and were trying to do the same with his successor Charles II! So Mary was executed for petty treason rather than witchcraft. It could have led to an unhappy spirit haunting that area, and the distinct possibility that the Spiritualist medium did actually get the name right without realising it, with the intervening changes in spelling and pronunciation which three and a half centuries can bring.

Of course, Oliver Cromwell, the 'Lord Protector', did not leave a good natural successor to his Puritan rule, and eventually the country welcomed Charles II back to the throne. There must have been some glum faces in Ipswich, but the Sparrowe family celebrated in style, rubbing their ex-captors noses in the changes that had come about. Around the Ancient House one can see some of the finest examples of pargetting, the decorative plasterwork typical of such wealthy houses from the period, overlooked by the enigmatic face carved into a beam overhanging the corner of Dial Lane opposite. There are religious symbols (such as the pelican pecking its own breast) and four continents named and illustrated beneath four windows. The fifth continent, 'Australasia', had not been discovered by Europeans yet. In the middle is a huge 1670s painted crest, with 'C II R' above it, the initials of the restored king, erected about a century after the house had been built. It has to have been the most rampant form of triumphalism at the time; in all its gaudy glory it proclaims that the Sparrowe family cause had been won at last.

Carved end beam on the corner of Dial Lane.

The Organists of St Stephen's

Opposite the Buttermarket entrance stands the attractive medieval fifteenth-century St Stephen's Church, which nowadays is home to the Tourist Information Office. It was used as a site office for the Buttermarket complex, and apparently some workers got a scare entering it alone. The ghosts that haunt it nowadays appear in the area to the left of the altar site at between 3 and 4 o'clock in the afternoon. Because it was the original location of the organ, the pair of female spooks are known as 'the organists'. They were reported by staff in the first few months of transferring there from the Town Hall in 1994, and have continued to appear for the last fifteen years or so.

In researching the Church I found that two ladies kept the place going after it lost its minister: two spinster sisters from 144 Woodbridge Road in Ipswich by the names of Ruby and Mimmie Humblestone. They cleaned, arranged flowers, played the organ and opened the Church each Sunday, however small the congregation. Eventually the Church authorities refused to fund the building any more. The sisters were devastated, and died not long afterwards. In telling the tale, visitors to our ghost tour have given us more details about them. A fishmonger told me how he sold them cheap fish on

Memorial in St Stephen's Church.

Saturday teatimes for their many cats. A florist said that they purchased flowers for the altar every Thursday. That they rescued stray cats was just one fact confirmed by their niece (who also came on the tour): she complained of the smell of the creatures in her aunties' house. She added that she was not at all surprised by them appearing at St Stephen's, since they spent so much time in the building. It is interesting to see that relatively recent deaths have produced ghosts, and that not every haunting has to be ancient and in outlandish costume. Ghosts must be created regularly, and just as regularly fade away when their purpose is met. Otherwise we wouldn't be able to move for them!

To the right of the organ space in which they frequently appear is an unusual coloured memorial decoration, dedicated to Robert Leman and his wife in 1637. It also shows their children. He was once Lord Mayor of London, but from the verse it appears as if he stayed close to his wife, even in death:

> Beneath this monument entombed lie
> A rare remark of a conjugal tye
> Robert and Mary, who to show how neere
> They did comply, How to each other deere
> One loathe behind the other long to stay
> (As Married) Died together in one day.

Soft Shoes Shuffling

I hear many stories, but do not believe them all. Many can be explained away by a trick of the light, genuine mistake, exaggeration or drunkenness. In general I do not repeat these type of tales, since I have lots of other stories I find more credible, but I will make an exception here and explain why I think this following tale may point to a ghost that was very convenient to the people who mentioned it.

Around the corner to the left from St Stephen's Lane in the Buttermarket road is a small shop that has changed owner several times. It was once a shoe shop, and I met two elderly ladies who retired from employment there when it closed. I asked them about the ghost that reportedly haunts the building. They looked at each other with a smile of conspiracy, but with gentle persuasion told me what happened there. They stated that there seemed to be something odd in the basement, and that the loo sometimes flushed by itself. They both preferred not to go down there. It happened to be where all the spare stock was stored.

'So what happened when a customer wanted something from down there, in a different size or colour?' I asked. They explained that the only other staff member, the male manager would go down, whilst they continued serving.

'So you did not have to troop up and down the stairs all day then?' I continued.

'No,' came the coy reply. 'And we worked there for many years together,' they added. I think that provided a very good reason for that ghost to exist!

The Running Man and Others

Further down, on the left of Buttermarket road there is a blind alley between two buildings, finishing in an emergency exit door from the rear of the Buttermarket complex. Before the complex was built, it cut between Cowells department store (famous for its extensive basement toy displays at Christmas) and Cowells printers. As a boy I used to love to see and hear the big printing machines thumping away, whilst their minders lounged at the big sash windows, and I sometimes asked them what they were printing. It could be anything from an Ipswich Town football programme to a poster for the mighty Co-op Fête. The lane used to continue on a dog-leg bend down through to the Old Cattle Market.

Every now and again, people would move aside to make way for a man running towards the Buttermarket. If they turned their heads to follow him, though, he faded before he reached the road. Nobody knows who the fleet-footed phantom was, or why he was running. Curiously, I have only ever had reports from people walking towards him, and none from those following behind. Since the alleyway has been blocked, he has ceased appearing. Maybe it is a ghost that has not learnt to run through walls?

Betty Puttick, in her 1998 book *Ghosts of Suffolk*, reported that several workers at J.S. Cowells' store witnessed the unearthly visitation of a monk. She also mentions a sealed underground chamber containing skeletons which was discovered during the

The alleyway of the 'running man'.

The café on Dial Lane.

construction of the Buttermarket complex there. Whether it related to the nearby Church graveyard of St Stephen or the Carmelite Priory is unknown.

Also on this section of the Buttermarket from St Stephen's Lane, beside Cowells store, there was a popular eating house called Limmers Restaurant. Staff were distraught to find that the ghost of the owner, Mr Limmer, still kept a sinister eye upon them, even after hanging himself on the top floor. Apparently he was a very fussy manager, with a pernickety attitude to detail, so maybe he continued to worry whether they were doing things correctly.

Across the Buttermarket from St Stephen's Lane lies Dial Lane. It was originally called Cookes Row, but a clock was erected extending out from the side of St Lawrence Church in 1844, suggesting a name change. It was taken down in 1882. (The Sparrowe family from the Ancient House are buried in a crypt below St Lawrence's Church.)

On the same side as this fifteenth-century Church is the Pickwick coffee house. It has an Art Deco frontage and reportedly houses a ghost, but the owners were reluctant to talk about it. The building used to be Scarborow Opticians, and you can still see a symbol of spectacles within the metalwork. In the narrow Churchyard itself, a visitor took a photograph of three small glowing orbs. It is true that these sometimes result from flecks of dust in the air or even light bouncing off a lens, but these were visible to the naked eye and moving fast in zig-zag patterns.

three

TAVERN STREET, TOWER STREET AND NORTHGATE STREET

The Riddles of Ridleys

At the end of Dial Lane turn right as you exit onto Tavern Street, one of the main shopping thoroughfares of Ipswich. There used to be a classy department store there called Ridleys, which traded for almost 100 years before closing in 1983. A pair of ladies who worked together there for many years used to come in early, before the store opened. One of the first tasks was to start up the boiler in the basement. One morning the first lady in descended to the basement, and soon heard heavy breathing. Thinking it was her colleague, out of breath from hurrying, she called out to her, but there was no reply. She realised that her friend had not yet arrived... She was later found much shaken, and refused to go down to the basement by herself ever again. Later that day, her colleague from the gents' outfitters department consoled her in the canteen. He confided that he had often seen a figure in the dress of a cavalier float right across his department floor in the middle of the afternoon. Up until then he had not told anyone for fear that he might be ridiculed, lose promotions or even his job. Those must be common reasons why ghosts in the workplace are under-reported. Continue along Tavern Street from Dial Lane, and turn left into Tower Street.

Geoffrey Chaucer (1343-1400), the author of *The Canterbury Tales*, is not made much of in his home town, but since he only mentioned Ipswich once when he commented upon its 'scheming conniving merchants', maybe that is not surprising. His own parents were merchants of a kind. The parents of Geoffrey Chaucer were vintners at a building on the corner of Tower Street, although there are disputes over which corner. It has sometimes been credited as being a tavern, and whilst that may be possible, there could be some confusion: vintners commonly sold or gave away glasses of wine as samples, so that customers could 'try before they buy.' If the wine was found to be acceptable, then a flagon, bottle or case was purchased. During excavations in the centre of Ipswich

Geoffrey Chaucer.

some old wells were found. One had been lined using many barrels with their tops and bottoms knocked out. The wooden-barrel remains of an Anglo-Saxon well in Greyfriars Street were later identified as coming from Mainz-am-Rhein; they were transported down the Rhine via the Dorestad trading centre before being shipped to Ipswich. By the number of these barrel remains found, wine from the Rhine in Germany must have been a popular tipple!

Acting Suspiciously?

The old Ipswich Arts Theatre (previously Poole's Picture Palace) is situated in Tower Street, although nowadays it is known as the Rep Bar (named for the great repertory company that once performed there). Local boy Sir Trevor Nunn progressed from here to worldwide theatrical fame, and his company contained many notable actors including John Southworth and Pam Ferris. They had their own theatrical ghost, who used to appear in the fourth or fifth row of the stalls whilst they were rehearsing. He was an old man in a coat and hat, and was always thought of as a good-luck omen, since there were good audiences and reviews after his visits. The theatre had one disadvantage – no connection between the back of stage left and stage right. The fairy queen may have appeared with soggy wings if she had to run outside and around the front of the theatre in winter! Since then the theatre company has moved to the New Wolsey Theatre on Civic Drive, and the building seen service as a costume store and a Church before conversion to a pub.

The old Ipswich Arts Theatre on Tower Street.

Further along the street on the same side as the theatre is No. 13, the Admirals House, built in the late seventeenth century. It is now part of the Ipswich Institute but was originally the home of Admiral Benjamin Page (1765-1845). He entertained the Duke of Wellington there in 1820, and donated maritime paintings to the Town Hall.

Burials

Turn right into Tower Churchyard Lane, and look at the grand St Mary Le Tower Church on your left, the centre for civic services. In 1200 the burghers of Ipswich received a charter there for a town market from King John, plus the 'great court trump', a trumpet which was once used to summon people to court. It can be seen in Ipswich Museum. It is likely that the town had a market before 1200, but King John hit on a money-making scheme to allow them to continue. It is thought that the old name for the town, Gippeswic, refers to a shore-side market on the land of Gippe (an Anglo-Saxon male name). The Church tower has the four gospel symbols at its corners: saints Matthew, Mark, Luke and John are respectively represented by a man, lion, ox and eagle.

Although it has a much larger Churchyard than many other town Churches, not all parishioners were buried in it. The wealthy would be buried in crypts below the Church, with less wealthy corpses being interred in the Churchyard. The top place there was in the east, since it was believed they would rise first on Judgement Day. No

St Mary Le Tower Church.

large gravestones were normally provided until Victorian times, and the dead were frequently buried above each other in layers, due to the shortage of space in what was a classy and commercially expensive neighbourhood. Inevitably graveyard levels in the town centre often rose over time, causing damp problems to the Church walls. Some had to have a small ditch dug around them to prevent the problem.

Some folk were not allowed to be buried in the Churchyard. Executed criminals were generally buried in unmarked graves on prison land, or at crossroads (presuming their body had not been hung in a gibbet cage to rot). Suicides were frowned on as cheating the day of death decided by God; they were buried outside the Church boundary in un-consecrated ground, as were the bodies of babies who died before being christened. So be wary as you step along the lane – you may not know who you are stepping upon... Continue past Hatton Court on your right, and round the corner into Oak Lane.

Unwelcome Guests at the White Horse Hotel

Between Tavern Street and Oak Lane is the famous Great White Horse Hotel, originally called simply The Tavern. The Georgian façade hides an older building once used to billet Parliamentary troops during the English Civil War. Nowadays Starbucks occupies part of the ground floor. In days gone by it was a well-known coaching inn on the Norwich to London route, with a central courtyard. Famous people stayed

The Great White Horse Hotel.

there, including King George II, King Louis XVIII of France and Charles Dickens. Dickens even set the breach of promise scene in *The Pickwick Papers* there. He used to visit the town to perform dramatic readings of his works, an art at which he displayed great talent. I wonder if he requested that his bed be set facing north to south? (He belonged to a society that believed that brain power was increased by sleeping with the head in the north and feet in the south, in line with magnetic lines of the earth. One might think it worked for him!) Dickens was one of the early members of The Ghost Club. I wonder if he was aware of the ghosts haunting this hotel? I am sure he would have found them fascinating.

Room 305 houses the ghost of a lady who walks across the room and through the wall. It is believed that it is the spirit of Flossie Fluyd (pronounced 'fluid') who died in the early 1920s during one of two serious fires at the hotel. The doorway was moved when the room was rebuilt, but she appears to still use the old location. Her presence is reported frequently, and noises are heard from the room when it is known to be empty.

Elsewhere in the hotel, Room 209 has a rather unique way of alarming the guests: they hear the sound of heavy furniture being dragged about in the room above them in the early hours of the morning. However, after one of those two fires there is no room above Room 209! There is only the roof. The staff have heard the complaints so often that they have learnt to ignore them.

There was a major investigation back in 2006 by John Blythe and friends. They reported the disembodied boots of a soldier walking along a back corridor. (One wonders how they knew the boots belonged to a soldier?) They also encountered the ghost of a servant girl – who they believe was murdered – and heard unexplained voices on a camcorder. They also heard a wheeled table 'dancing around the ballroom'.

Charles Dickens, a more welcome visitor to the Great White Horse Hotel.

Wayland Smith carving on the corner post of Oak House nearby.

Pykenham Gate, Northgate Street.

Nasty Doings in Northgate Street: Oak House

As you get to the end of Oak Lane, on its left corner with Northgate Street, you reach the splendid late fifteenth-century Oak House, formerly Oak Inn. It has a fine collection of stained glass and wood panelling. Not all of it is original. One owner used to tour Ipswich demolition sites and save good-quality features to incorporate into the building, rather than let them be destroyed. Maybe he imported something else as well, as a legal secretary working there now told me that the basement (probably once the beer cellar) has an eerie feel to it and she will not retrieve files from it if working alone. As you enter Northgate Street, look at the old carved corner post of the building, with the eroded figure of blacksmith and local legend Wayland Smith.

Pykenhams Gatehouse

Carry on up Northgate Street (site of an old town ditch and bank boundary, most likely constructed during the Viking occupation of the town in the late ninth or early tenth century) and you will reach Archdeacon Pykenham's Gatehouse, built in 1471. The building (now occupied by the Ipswich and Suffolk Club) replaced the one owned by the absentee Cardinal of St Angelo in Rome, who drew fees from ecclesiastical courts without bothering to visit them. The original building was ransacked in the Peasants Revolt of June 1381. Apparently, although Archdeacon Pykenham did live locally, he was not much better than Angelo. A contemporary called Robert Thorpe of Hadleigh (where Pykenham also built the Deanery Tower in 1495) said that Pykenham was 'neither worshipful nor virtuous' and he was reportedly dishonest in a couple of transactions. The Hadleigh Deanery itself was never completed and Archdeacon Pykenham died two years later. Does his ghost frequent there still? I don't know, but a couple of people have mentioned feeling 'a presence' upstairs in this delightful building, now home to the Ipswich and Suffolk Club.

Pykenhams Gatehouse has spikes over the gates, and is sometimes mistakenly thought to be the north gate of Ipswich after which the street is named. The real North Gate (or St Margaret's Bar Gate), which was demolished in 1794, stood at the end of Northgate Street, and had much larger spikes on to hold the severed heads of those criminals the town particularly reviled. They were sometimes dipped in tar to preserve them longer, as a sort of warning not to commit crimes to people entering the town by this route. (Somewhat more effective one suspects than those modern Neighbourhood Watch signs.)

Mcgintys – The Most Haunted Building in Ipswich

Beyond Pykenham's Gatehouse is a pub originally known as the Halberd Inn, (similar to a Beefeaters pike axe weapon) but nowadays as McGintys Irish theme pub. I believe it is the most haunted place in Ipswich; it has been visited by programmes for both

The Halberd Inn, nowadays called McGintys.

BBC and ITV. It is built at what was the corner of the town boundary, and has a fragment of the wall incorporated in its structure. When alterations were made to the pub, a well was rediscovered beneath the floor, with water still flowing. It has had a wall erected around it since and can be seen just inside the door.

One thick sidewall borders on a lane leading to the Tower Ramparts, once an important part of the town defences. People leaning their head on that wall inside the pub during quiet periods have heard the sound of a human heartbeat throbbing from within.

The man who originally converted the pub to an Irish theme was Harold, a short and pleasant Irishman. One night he closed the bar and escorted two barmaids to the taxi office up the road. He had left his mother-in-law, who was visiting, alone inside. By the time he returned she had barricaded herself into a corner of the pub, frightened of the noise of footsteps on stairs beyond the open fireplace. She knew that there was nobody else in the pub. She also knew that the staircase had been taken down many years before!

Another time, Harold awoke at around 2 a.m., and heard noises downstairs. Fearing a break in, he picked up a baseball bat and walked down the stairs in his pyjamas. There did not appear to be any windows broken or doors forced, and he could not find anyone hiding. However, to his surprise he found ten shot glasses smashed at regular intervals in a line parallel to the front of the bar. Puzzled, he went back to bed. Waking with a clearer head he remembered the CCTV he had recently installed, and examined the footage (which he later showed to me). It flicks from one scene to another around the pub, with a time signature displayed in the bottom left corner. You must remember that the only light came from subdued security lighting plus a street light shining through the windows. One frame shows the area in front of the bar, with a pool of light on the carpet from the window. Twenty seconds later, according to the time coding, one can see two black smudges in that light. Harold told me that this was the centre of the line of broken glasses. They can be seen in shot for the rest of the footage. Eventually one can see Harold stalking into the bar in pyjamas with his baseball bat. (The subject of much mirth at his expense.) Finally he is seen going back up the stairs.

Even if someone had hidden in the bar, I would find it inconceivable that they could smash ten glasses in a line and hide themselves effectively in the twenty seconds that elapsed from one camera shot to the next. It remains a mystery, along with many other phenomena at the pub.

One evening I led a party to the pub, expecting to meet my colleague Ed. He was sitting in the covered courtyard with one of his staff, talking, when the staff member saw a shadow moving along the wall. She assumed it was me arriving – but when she looked around the corner there was no one there. A few minutes later I arrived with my group and was told laughingly about the shadow. One of my party then told me that, after the stables were no longer needed, the area had been made into a skittle alley, and then into a range for air-pistol shooting. He remembered coming to the club with his dad as a young boy. Sometimes, he recalled, all shooting in the range would be stopped after a shadow was seen moving on the wall near the door – but nobody could ever be found. In the end they roped off the end lane to ensure there were no accidents. He had thought that everyone knew about it, but it was news to me, and fortunate that he should happen to be on the tour the very night it re-occurred.

The pub has changed hands a couple of times since Harold, but each owner talks about staff (who are often over from Ireland) staying in one particular bedroom who have experienced sudden draughts, eerie sounds and the bedclothes being pulled off them in the night. Vanessa, the current landlady, allowed us to keep vigil one Hallowe'en. She had mentioned that barrels seemed to move in the cellar. One keen person sprinkled talcum powder all around, and the door was locked. In the early hours, noises were heard emanating from the cellar. On unlocking and entering, it was noted that a heavy, full beer barrel had moved over six inches in the talc. No footmarks or handprints were found.

Vanessa's predecessor had an experience one night when the entire electrics failed totally, despite there being several separate circuits and fuses. The electrician who called found no particular cause for this to happen to the whole system, but did find a single bit of equipment which had developed a fault. The casing was live, and could easily have killed anyone touching it. Maybe the failure was caused by the reportedly helpful spirit of a monk reputed to haunt the place: a medium once declared that the monk had been murdered whilst shielding another person from an attack.

Panic at Pipers Court

Opposite McGintys, Great Colman Street leads to a block of flats converted from the old Phillips & Piper Ltd clothing factory (1859-1981) named Pipers Court, which has in a short time had several suicides and a murder on the premises. It has an underground car park, and a security man who patrols the building. A child was sometimes seen playing in the car park, but always disappeared before he could be apprehended. One night a security guard got a bit closer, and thought he would see how he had eluded capture. He got his answer when the boy ran straight through the wall. Shocked, the guard told his company he was no longer willing to patrol there. Fortunately, another employee wanted a transfer, so they swapped posts. The new man tells me he sees nothing down there but cars, and is quite glad of it.

Nearly opposite used to stand a leather tanning factory. I once met a pensioner who had worked there as a young girl. They had a rush order on for some saddle leather, and a young man, soon to be married, jumped at the chance of some overtime after his other workmates had gone home for the day. Unfortunately he was overwhelmed by the noxious fumes, and his body was found half slumped into the tanning vat the next morning. Some staff continued to see his melancholy ghost, and shortly afterwards the owners closed the place down, still very upset at what had happened.

Pipers Court, Great Colman Street.

four

CHRIST CHURCH PARK AREA

Peril at the Packhorse Inn

On the opposite side of St Margaret's Plain from McGintys, on the corner of Soane Street, is an old building. Formerly the Packhorse Inn, it is currently an estate agent. It dates back to the seventeenth century, and was built on the site of the Anglo-Saxon Thingstead, a place where trial by ordeal would have been carried out as well as council meetings. (The accused may have been expected to carry a red-hot iron bar for several paces. If the burns did not heal cleanly he would be presumed guilty.) The inn was altered drastically in the twentieth century for road widening. One alteration was the demolition of an external staircase on the side facing Tower Ramparts. However, a few late-night pedestrians saw the back of a figure in a dark red shirt walk up the invisible stairs!

Old Packhouse Inn, corner of Soane Street and Old Foundry Road.

The Christchurch Mansion Characters

Across Soane Street from the Packhorse Inn and the Freemasons Hall is the grand main entrance to Christchurch Park and Mansion. The origins of the building go back to Henry VIII's Dissolution of the Monasteries. The Augustinian Holy Trinity Priory of Black Canons built in 1160 was suppressed in 1537 (some ruins can be seen) and the Withypoll family bought the land in 1545, building a mansion there. The heart of the building is an Elizabethan 'E' form in red brick, with several later additions. Queen Elisabeth I visited twice, and King Charles II visited Viscount Hereford and played bowls here. Beyond the mansion stands a monument to nine Protestant martyrs burnt on the Cornhill between the years 1555–1558.

It was later acquired in the eighteenth century by Claude Fonnereau, a London merchant of Huguenot descent. Nowadays it is a museum, and holds a fine collection of art (including East Anglian works by Gainsborough and Constable). It is in the upstairs picture gallery that the ghost I would most like to see in Ipswich manifests. I have heard reports from three independent sources, and each informant has emphasised how charming this particular apparition is. It is a lady described as being in her late twenties to early thirties. Her hair is piled up, and she wears a long, straight, possibly Edwardian dress. She holds the hands of two children in her own, and they are dancing round. Although no sound is heard, she is leaning backwards and clearly laughing. One old gent who saw the scene told me he wished he was an artist, commenting 'If I could capture that scene I would sell a thousand copies!'

Downstairs has a Grey Lady ghost of an earlier period, who sweeps by in a wide, floor-length gown. I wonder if she is the same lady frequently seen at No. 11 Soane Street, near to the sixteenth-century Running Buck pub? An old friend of mine called Avril used to visit the Stollery family there in the 1950s. Mr Stollery was a motor engineer, and Avril was a teenage friend of his daughter. A grey ghostly lady used

Christchurch Mansion.

to sweep through their sitting room from the park side of the house to the street. Unusually, if one was close enough you could feel the 'swish' as she moved past.

There is one other ghost reported in Christchurch Mansion, that of a servant girl who died mysteriously. She was investigated by Richard Keeble and Paul Moss-Kemp of the Society for Psychical Research.

The Purple Shop

Around the corner from Soane Street, Fonnereau Road (named after the ex-owners of the mansion) runs alongside the park boundary. The Purple Shop (founded in 1971) is on its corner with Tower Ramparts. I used to know the ex-owner, Tommo, and his wife before they retired. Tommo was a very straightforward sort of a chap, but had two unexplained stories.

He and his wife liked the radio on in their shop. At the end of the day they would switch it off, lock the door and go upstairs to their flat. Frequently, the radio would already be on when they emerged downstairs the next morning. They never saw a ghost, but presumed if there was one it was musical. We shall meet Tommo again in St Nicholas Street…

The Purple Shop, Fonnereau Road.

The St George Street Spectre

At the other end of Crown Street and the Tower Ramparts bus station, a footpath leads to St George Street, named after the old St George's Chapel that once stood there. Mrs Amelia Cobb, the mother of an old friend, told me about the chilling ghost she encountered living there as a young girl. It was at No. 53, a house which was rebuilt after a serious fire. This denizen of the Otherworld was believed to be a lady ex-resident who perished in the inferno, trying to retrieve a money box from under her bed. Amelia reported to me that she had the covers pulled off her bed more than once by an unknown force.

The Rainbow pub once stood on the corner of St George Street and St Matthews Street. The licensee was murdered on the premises, and the place was shunned by many after that because of what was described as 'a bad atmosphere'. The building was demolished in 1961.

Beware the Woolpack Inn

Retrace your steps and cross diagonally opposite across Christchurch Park from the Purple Shop to the old sixteenth-century Woolpack Inn of Tuddenham Road. There was a tollgate nearby at one time, so some thrifty folk would stable their horses and abandon wagons along the road to avoid paying charges. It has long held a spooky reputation, and the landlord's dog steadfastly refused to enter the cellar. A medium called Sue Knock planned to hold a psychic evening there, and put up a large card poster on the wall advertising it. The next night two of the regulars pointed at it and laughed. They stopped laughing when it dropped from the wall by itself though!

Of course it could have been a coincidence, but Sue claims that the ghost of Admiral Vernon, who died in 1757, dwells there, far from his home in the village of Nacton. He was known as 'Old Grog' (from the French grogram sea cloak he habitually wore), and gave his name to the watered rum ration he gave to his sailors. It also had citrus juice added, and this drastically decreased the number of sailors falling ill with scurvy, caused by a deficiency of vitamin C. He is best remembered for his victories in the War of Jenkins Ear between 1739 and 1748. A merchant captain, Robert Jenkins, claimed that Spanish coastguards had cut off his ear in a dispute, and produced the grizzly evidence before the British Parliament. Admiral Vernon captured the important silver trading port of Portobello on 22 November 1739. On his triumphant return to England he was fêted as a hero, and at a celebratory dinner in 1742 the song 'Rule Britannia' was first sung.

The ethereal Admiral Vernon was not short of ghostly company at the Woolpack. A startled chef saw a grey figure pass through his bedroom, and Sue Knock also claimed that there was a headless monk, a drowned seaman, and the spirit of a publican called George. Additionally there are stories of a Catholic priest suffocated whilst hiding in a barrel and a seaman with a ponytail that walked straight through landlord Stuart Appleby!

If you now walk down Bolton Lane you will come to St Margaret's Green.

The Woolpack, Tuddenham Road.

Manor House, St Margaret's Plain.

Margaret at the Manor House

On St Margaret's Plain, the Manor House Club was once the home of the Cobbold brewing family. A servant, Margaret Catchpole (1762-1819), saved their child from drowning in a pond at the rear, earning their eternal gratitude – even after she was transported for horse stealing. Escaping gaol, she was sent to Australia as a convict. The family sent her a sewing kit to establish her as a needlewoman on her release. A ghost of a woman in the Manor Club startled builders completing renovations there, but it is unlikely to be Margaret, as she died in Australia.

In earlier times the house was home to Nathaniel Bacon, a leading lawyer and Chairman of the Eastern Association Committee for the Puritans in the English Civil War.

St Margaret's Plain (sometimes also called St Margaret's Green) used to be the site of the Holy Rood Fair, held each year on 25-27 September. Originally granted to the nearby Priory of Holy Trinity in the twelfth century, it reverted to the Crown, and then to the Withypoll family (of Christchurch Mansion) in the sixteenth century, but it was restored to Ipswich Corporation in a 1665 charter from Charles II. The fair principally sold cheese, butter, sausages and sweetmeats and was last held in 1844.

Turn left past the Manor House onto St Margaret's Street and cross the entrance to Woodbridge Road into St Helen's Street.

five

ST HELEN'S STREET AREA

The Relic in the Regent Theatre

Known to older Ipswich residents as the Gaumont (a name it had as a cinema/theatre for many years) the venue in St Helen's Street now concentrates on live shows. However, a less lively private show can sometimes be seen upstairs as a ghost lady walks through the entrance into the circle seating area. She has been seen by several of the ushers. When I used to go backstage to do interviews for a local paper, one of the technicians swore that someone or something lived beneath the stage, 'and it makes more noise than a cornered rat!'

An Inconvenient Ghost

A little further along St Helen's Street, on the opposite side to the Regent, once stood a popular Shanks bakery. The staff had to go upstairs to use the loo, and sometimes found that the door would not open, despite nobody else occupying the smallest room at the time. At least one shop assistant felt a sense of foreboding and also saw a shadowy figure in the gloom of the upstairs corridor. The shop was well known for delivering sandwiches and cakes to nearby businesses, long before the modern establishment of such trade. It led to the humorous repetition of the well-known phrase that greeted the pedestrian bearer of the food: 'Oh, delivered by Shanks Pony!' (The phrase is a colloquial one usually meaning to walk, and refers to the portion of the leg between the ankle and knee, rather than the bakery name.)

The County of Suffolk Pub

Further along St Helen's Street from the Regent, and formerly called the County Hotel (and before that the Bear & Crown) is the County of Suffolk pub; you may

The County of Suffolk pub.

notice that the windows are all angled to view the keep left bollard on a concrete triangle at the bottom of Orchard Street. This gives a hint of the grisly secret of the building's past. It was the site of public hangings from the old county court and jail opposite: people would actually hire a room so that they and their friends could get a good view – something akin to booking an executive box at a concert or sporting event.

In the early 1820s there were around 200 capital offences for which you could be hanged, including wearing a mask at a burglary, stealing cloth and poaching. Many of these offences were removed from the list in 1823.

There was one particular hanging that attracted an enormous amount of attention. In 1844, fifty-one-year-old Mary Shemmings of Martlesham was accused of the murder of one of her grandchildren by poisoning. Her twenty-one-year-old daughter Caroline had two illegitimate children, and it was said that Mary was fed up of being left to look after them. After the baby died, someone remembered Mary buying arsenic (at that time sold openly to combat rats). A local carpenter was also heard to say that she ordered a coffin three days before the death – which, if true, would seem a bit of a giveaway! The sad little body was exhumed from Waldringfield Meeting House graveyard and the inquest was held at Martlesham Red Lion (which she is reputed to haunt). She was found guilty at the County Court in Bury St Edmunds, but returned to Ipswich. She was hanged by the executioner Calcraft on Saturday 11 January 1845, in front of a crowd of 10,000 people. She was the first woman to be hanged at Ipswich for thirty years. Later that same month, twenty-eight-year-old William Howell was hanged on the 25th for the murder of a policeman, Constable John McFadden, who had tried to arrest him and his gang of farm rustlers. Two other gang members were transported to Australia, a common alternative to hanging at the time.

Public hangings ended in 1868, and the last one in Ipswich was the execution of black-hearted murderer John Ducker in April 1863, who was hanged for killing a policeman in Halesworth. By the time that Henry Bedingfield was hanged on 3 December 1879 (for murdering his mistress in a fit of jealous rage) the executions were conducted inside the prison in front of a select number of witnesses.

Jealousy was also the motive for factory worker and former Coldstream Guard Thomas Day, who traced Caroline Meek, his ex-lover and mother to his illegitimate child Lillian, from Birmingham to Station Road, Ipswich – where she had married another man. He cut the throat of Lillian as she sat on his lap. He was hanged on Tuesday 13 November 1883 by executioner Bartholomew Binns. Young rapist George Nunn of Wortham killed his thirty-three-year-old victim, Eliza Dixon, a mother of six, with fourteen stab wounds, and paid the ultimate price on Tuesday 21 November 1899. From these few examples, one can see that hanging for murder was still reasonably infrequent in Victorian Ipswich – five cases in just over fifty years. Despite what modern newspapers may say, I think that it was far more dangerous on the streets back then than it is now.

The last execution in Ipswich was on 27 November 1924, of a farm labourer called Southgate from Ardleigh who had murdered his wife.

Inevitably, with such fiendish associations, it isn't surprising that the pub may be haunted. The cellar is subject to strange noises, and people who visit it alone report feeling frightened by the atmosphere in there. However, the main haunting is reckoned to be a male spirit who haunts the upstairs. Maybe he is someone 'who had one for the road'. With an eye to business, landlords of pubs would sometimes offer a drink to those on their way to execution (which meant, of course, that people would buy drinks at their pub to see the condemned man). That is the way that expression came into popular usage.

The County Hall, Court and Jail

The court was moved to this site from the Cornhill in about 1786; in 1936 it heard the divorce case of Wallis Simpson, later to marry Edward VIII. Edward abdicated the throne of Great Britain in what became a very public and very controversial scandal.

The jail was built to radical new principles, influenced by the work of penal reformer John Howard, with males divided from females, and a separate debtor's prison. In the 1800s it was amongst the first prisons to have a tread-wheel installed. The tread-wheel was designed by the Suffolk engineer Cubitt to wear out prisoners. Margaret Catchpole was imprisoned here and escaped with the aid of Will Laud, her lover.

The buildings ended up as the headquarters of Suffolk County Council, who left in 2006. During that time, the old condemned cell was used as a paper store. An employee who used to scoff at anything he regarded as 'un-scientific' once went in there to

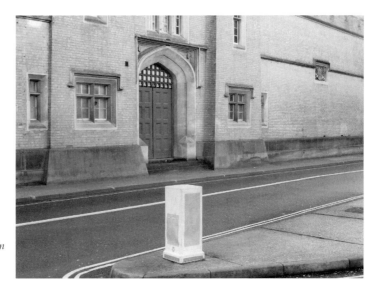

Old County Hall, St Helen's Street. The bollard in the foreground is where the public gallows once stood.

get some photocopy paper. He came out much shaken, and accused his colleagues of 'setting him up'. He would not say what had happened, but in future was very reluctant to go back. It was later re-utilised as a multi-faith chapel.

Sacred Earth

Around the corner from St Helen's Street (almost opposite to the Regent) into Upper Orwell Street, two old friends, Anthony Moorhouse and Nigel Pearson, have run the esoteric shop Sacred Earth since 1991. When they moved into No. 6 some years ago (the shop is now at No. 8), they became acquainted with a spirit they called Edwin. They had no aversion to him, and would greet him each morning, and ask him to keep an eye on things when they left at night. Mostly they sensed rather than saw him. They agreed that his favourite spot seemed to be a corner of the back wall upstairs. His one foible was sending the pictures crooked, and they gave up straightening the pictures and therapist certificates that they hung there.

The pair bought a puppy with the intention of keeping him in the shop. The day before he arrived, a late and large delivery of stock had been made. They had left the packing materials all over the floor upstairs. The next morning Nigel tucked the animal inside his jacket, carried it up the steep wooden stairs and placed it on the floor to explore. He expected the dog to play with the packing paper; instead it walked straight over to Edwin's corner, sat down, wagged its tail and then settled down for a doze. It repeated the behaviour each morning, suggesting that dogs and other small animals may be better than adults at detecting the presence of the supernatural. Nobody has told them not to be stupid or make up lies.

Go along Upper Orwell Street a short distance from Sacred Earth and you will find an alleyway on your left called Upper Orwell Court. Walk through it to Bond Street.

Sacred Earth and Absolution shops, Orwell Street.

It was named after Henry Cooper Bond, who once had a tannery there. His house was at Major's Corner (where the Regent Theatre now stands), far enough from the smell of the tannery but near enough to walk to work. Opposite you will see an old Ragged School of Ipswich. We shall see another one soon, and discover more about them. Turn right along Bond Street, and on your right, just before Eagle Street, you will see an old fire station converted into flats.

Fear at the Old Fire Station

The Ipswich Fire Brigade, formed in 1875 and originally quartered in nearby Waterworks Street, moved to Bond Street in 1899. Even when a larger, more modern fire station was created on Valley Road it remained as a sub-station for many years. It has now converted to more student accommodation.

Some students are happy to live there, but others leave after a few weeks, disturbed by horrid dreams and unexplained noises. An old fireman told me that in its heyday the firemen themselves talked of a ghost. The history is a tragic one. One of their colleagues was doing some maintenance in the yard when the alarm went off for a 'shout'. He should have joined the crew, but his friend said he'd take his place. It was a factory fire, and as the fire brigade fought to bring it under control a wall collapsed, killing the man instantly. His colleague back at the station was very upset, and became depressed; he should have been the one to die, he thought. He hanged himself in an upstairs room of the station. It was closed soon after that, with services transferred to other fire stations.

Spread Eagle, Eagle Street.

The Whisperers of Eagle Street

At the other end of Bond Street, you meet a crossroads of Rope Walk and Eagle Street. Turn right into Eagle Street, which provides us with a dark haul of mystery, as well as the home at No. 9 of radical social historian John Glyde (1823-1905).

A little further up the street, on the left-hand side, are a set of student flats over a shop. I was invited there once, and asked to see if I could detect anything of a psychic nature. I wandered into each of the three student's rooms, and found nothing uncommon in them. Each time I stepped back onto the central staircase, though, it felt very different. It wasn't sinister, just not the same atmosphere as the rooms. Back in the kitchen with the students, over a cup of tea, I told them my feelings. 'It is the right place,' one confirmed, 'but did you hear anything?' I had to admit I had not. They then revealed that two of them had heard whispering or chattering behind them on the stairs, when they knew full well that no one else was in the building.

At the end of Eagle Street on that side is the Spread Eagle pub, which has an unspecified wraith whose story remains lost to us at present. It was once one of four pubs on the corners of that crossroads, the others being the Bulls Head, the Eclipse and the Shoulder of Mutton.

A Poltergeist

Along the opposite side of Eagle Street there is a double-fronted shop, next to the café on the corner. It used to be two separate shops, and back in the late 1930s the left-hand one became a restaurant. It was run by a couple with their teenage daughter, and right from the start they had problems. Cruets, cutlery and even plates went flying across the room. No ghost was seen, as is generally the case with poltergeist activity. Poltergeist

Poltergeist site, Eagle Street.

means 'noisy ghost' in German, and they are associated with physical movement of objects. There is a theory that they are the manifestation of surplus psychic energy from a disturbed adolescent. Certainly there was an adolescent on the premises, and most in my experience are disturbed!

After a few months the family got fed up and sold the lease onto some other people, who knew about the stories in the local press but did not believe them. The cynics soon had to change their minds though when the activity started up again. They tried an exorcist, but to no avail. Once again the place closed, and nobody local wanted it. My parents used to sarcastically say, 'I suppose the ghost of Eagle Street done that' if a breakage or spillage occurred without an explanation.

Another family from London (who supposedly did not know the local legend) finally took the place on, and the trouble started up all over again. The culmination of events happened at around 3 p.m. in the afternoon in front of a dozen people. An empty table juddered across the floor from one side of the café to the other. The shop was boarded up, and remained so through the war years and into the 1960s. I knew which one it was because my dad had once told me that tramps slept there (which makes an impression on a little boy). Then someone bought the place as well as the next-door shop and knocked them into one with a single central door. I have noticed that no business ever lasts long there. Other shops in the street seem to do well, particularly from people walking through to the nearby Suffolk University College.

One night I told the story to a group that included two Dutch female students. Afterwards, one of them explained that the other lived in a flat above the shop. Despite it being cheaper and nearer to the college than any of the more expensive alternatives, she was moving out because 'she just doesn't feel comfortable with the feel of the place.' Up until then she knew nothing of the events downstairs. As I am writing this book new owners have taken up residence, and returned it to being a café. On their heads be it!

This isn't the only site for a poltergeist in Eagle Street. A photograph of an unspecified Ipswich house appeared in the *Illustrated London News* of 27 December 1952 with the caption: 'A real-life Christmas "Ghost" story: Canon Harvey exorcising a "Poltergeist" in the home of Mr and Mrs Cecil Wilson (Eagle Street, Ipswich) while a police constable holds the evidence (a cribbage board).'

There has been other reported poltergeist activity in Ipswich: another café in St Margaret's Street was cleared by a priest, but a flat above a shop in Foxhall Road was less easily calmed when a medium visited in 2004. As well as physical movement of objects the sound of a baby crying and shadowy figures were noted.

The 'Orrible 'Ead.

On the right-hand side of Eagle Street at No. 11 there is a grotesque face over a door. A tale is told about its legendary origins. The area was originally desolate and swampy, and home only to a fierce ogre. The council needed to expand the town, but everything they built on the land by day the huge creature would break by night: the timbers were broken, the walls and roofs smashed. Eventually, a deputation was sent to try and bargain with the ogre. After long and difficult negotiations the ogre agreed to let them use the land provided that they carved an image of his head in the street to remind everyone whose land they were on. 'If ever you take my image down, I will come and take the whole street down, in one night!' he roared. That is why there is still the 'Orrible 'Ead of Eagle Street. Rumours that the dark, horrible, evil-smelling place he was sent to was Norwich are probably a good indicator of Suffolk's prejudice against its Norfolk neighbour…

The 'Orrible 'Ead, No. 11 Eagle Street.

The Lonely Fate of the Blue Coat Boy

Turn back up Eagle Street and turn right into Waterworks Street, which was originally called Dunghill Pound Lane, referring to a communal rubbish heap and place for storing stray animals. On the right is another old Ragged School, converted into housing. It is the site of a sad tale of the Blue Coat Boy, who used to be pictured on an Old Cattle Market pub sign.

There were originally four Ragged Schools in Ipswich. The other two were in Smart Street and St Matthews Street. Two were Blue Coat schools, two Grey Coat, due to the uniform that was given to distinguish the children from their more fortunate peers. The two pairs of schools resulted mainly from the work of John Gibbon and John Pemberton around 1717–18 in Ipswich. They were run by different groups of Churches to enable children whose parents were poor to have some basic education, along with an emphasis on religious studies and corporal punishment. The pupils did receive some lunch, such as soup and a roll.

During one winter the schoolmaster announced a holiday. Most pupils were pleased but one lad hated going home on payday, as his father would come home drunk from the pub, having spent most of his wages, and beat the child's mother and his siblings. The small child planned to hide in the school instead. He had not realised that the holiday was for two weeks, not two days… The small fire had been left to go out, the food cupboard was empty and the school had been locked. There was no water since the school fetched it from a pump (they could not afford to pay for piped supplies). The waif was already thin and malnourished, and dressed in ragged clothing. He could

Ragged School, Waterworks Street.

Dragon carving,
Dedham Place.

not escape. His parents did not think to look for him at the school, and may have wondered if he had run off to find his fortune on a ship from Ipswich Docks, as many others did. When he was eventually found, a fortnight later, he had succumbed to the thirst, hunger and cold. A chair had been pulled up beneath the high-set windows (provided to prevent daydreaming), but it was thought that he would have been unable to reach much more than a finger to it due to his height. He was not forgotten, though, since at quiet times his pathetic whimpering for help continued to be heard, and sometimes a wraith in a blue coat was glimpsed, as sombre as the grave.

Here Be Dragons

Take the little-used Dedham Place public lane that passes down the left-hand side of the Ragged School building and out between 25-27 Fore Street. There is a wrought-iron gate at the far end, but just before it a wooden archway. Look on the Fore Street side and you will spot two beautifully carved dragons. People do not usually associate Suffolk with dragon stories, but in a document held by Canterbury Cathedral in Kent there is a description of an event taking place on the Suffolk/Essex border at Ballingdon Hill near Sudbury. A Black Dragon of Suffolk was seen to fight in the air with a mottled red and black creature from Essex. They eventually broke off and returned to their own lands. It is unusual to have such legends dated so precisely, but this indecisive battle was allegedly fought on 26 September, 1449, which is the date of my birthday, but a year or two out…

Turn left at the end of the alleyway onto Fore Street.

six

SALTHOUSE STREET AND THE DOCK AREA

If you cross the busy Star Lane at the end of Fore Street, you come to a cul-de-sac just before Fore Street Baths of what remains of Angel Lane. (This short lane once had three pubs to cure the thirsts of dock workers and sailors in it: the Angel, Duke of Edinburgh and the Lion & Lamb!) Look over towards the redundant fourteenth / fifteenth-century St Clement's Church, built as a 'sailor's Church' on the site of the earlier one dedicated to the unknown St Osterbolt. The Churchyard appropriately contains a memorial to Slade, the Royal Naval Architect who designed HMS *Victory* for Nelson, and who was responsible for developing the seventy-four gun ships for the Royal Navy after examining a similar captured French ship. Appropriately the Lord Nelson pub is nearby, and somewhere in this area is the lost site of the East Gate of Ipswich.

A Spontaneous Human Combustion

All around the world, over several centuries, there have been stories of spontaneous human combustion (where a person goes up in flames but the area around them is not burnt). The feet of the victim often survive, as in a well-documented and photographed case from South America. Ipswich has its very own story in this genre, here in Angel Lane on 9 April 1744.

A fisherman's wife, Mrs Pett, lived there. She had two grown-up daughters, one of whom was married and lived abroad. One summer's day, when her husband was away fishing, her daughter from abroad returned to Ipswich with her husband. Together with the other daughter they went out for a celebratory meal. At the end of the evening the couple from abroad retired to one of the many inns in the dockside area, whilst mother and her other daughter went home to Angel Lane.

On arising in the morning, the girl found a ghastly sight waiting for her downstairs: the ashes of her mother's trunk lay in the chair, with just her feet remaining. When her husband was away the mother often had trouble sleeping, and she sometimes came down to sit in a chair by the embers of the fire. Being summer, and as they had all been out, no fire had been lit. However, the woman habitually smoked a pipe, something quite common then. Although she was reduced to ash, the chair and area around her were only slightly charred. Thus did Ipswich get its own story of spontaneous human combustion. (Legend has a rather unlikely explanation for this event, ascribing it to a local farmer who, believing Mrs Pett was a witch who had cursed his flock, was advised to burn a live pig which had been given her name. He did so, and the rest is history…)

A 1998 QED TV documentary has shown, with the aid of a dead pig dressed in clothes, that reducing a body to ashes with a single flame is possible. The clothes were set on fire, and a large flame immediately leapt up. It would have been enough to suffocate a living person (or to cause a heart attack). After a few minutes the flame decreased to no more than the size of a match flame, which spread over the area exposed to the air. The original large flame had melted fat under the skin, which was drawn up by the heat into the clothes – which in turn acted as a wick. The effect is of an inside-out candle, with increasingly more of the body being consumed from without. In the experiment, the pig took about six hours to turn to ash, and all that remained unconsumed by the fire was the pig's trotters, which, just like human feet, have very little fat on them. It may sound like something out of the *X Files*, but I believe that this may be a reasonable explanation of what happens in some of these cases.

If I told you the case was written about by a journalist who visited the town, you might think, 'So what?' However, the journalist was one Charles Dickens, and he later used the story as inspiration for a part of his 1852 book *Bleak House* in which Krook, an alcoholic, perishes from such a cause. It was a commonly held belief at the time that spontaneous human combustions were fuelled by quantities of alcohol that the victim had previously consumed.

This was not current reporting, as has been claimed elsewhere. Dickens was not born until 1812, so could hardly have reported on a 1744 event as it happened! He claimed to have investigated about thirty such stories when challenged about the episode in his book.

Fiendish Fore Street

Turning left out of Angel Lane again into Fore Street (the 'foremost' street at the time), the seventeenth-century Lord Nelson pub still trades with sailors from the docks, but these are more likely to be yachting types than the sea salts of old. One such salt was Thomas Eldred. He took part in the second British circumnavigation (after Drake) of the world (along with Cavendish) between 1586-8. Thomas lived further along Fore Street at No. 97 (now demolished). That section of street seems a home for heroes. Edith Maud Cook is recorded as living at No. 90, now the Neptune Café. She made over 300 balloon flights, and was the first recorded British female aeroplane pilot in 1910. After several successful jumps from balloons she died in a tragic parachute accident later in that same year.

The Lord Nelson Apparition

The Lord Nelson pub was originally called the Noah's Ark, but later renamed in honour of the East Anglian hero who, in 1800, was elected to High Steward of Ipswich. He had a house in the appropriately named Victory Road. Apparently, his wife Frances (née Nisbet) headed for there from London once, hearing her husband was landing at Great Yarmouth, and wishing to surprise him. It turned out to be an unpleasant surprise for both of them, as he had arranged to rendezvous with his mistress (and later second wife) Emma Hamilton! When she heard, and in an understandable ill-temper, Frances removed all the bedclothes, servants and food back to London, so that he had to change his plans and stay at the Great White Horse instead.

When some alterations were being carried out upstairs at the Lord Nelson two mummified mice were discovered, smoke-dried between the floorboards and ground-floor ceiling. Also there were some fragments of glass bottles, often used to try and hamper their progress. When examined, the glass was found to be from the 1600s, and the relics of both mice and bottles can be seen in a display cabinet. They are not the only mysterious 'treasures' to be found upstairs, as you shall read.

The Lord Nelson pub once employed the famous transportee Margaret Catchpole in the kitchen (*see* The Manor Ballroom). Margaret had an adventurous life. One John Luff once tried to kill her and shove her down the well at the back of the Lord Nelson; she fought back and survived after a crowd of customers, hearing her screams, came to her aid. Luff wanted information about Will Laud, Margaret's partner, but did not want to be captured (as there was a price on his head). He died from an excise man's bullet a fortnight later.

There is a lady who brought her office Christmas party to the Lord Nelson one January afternoon after the madness of the season had passed. At the end of the meal the landlord enquired if everything was alright, and they all agreed the meal was splendid – but she added that it was made more entertaining for her by the appearance of a small child at the end of their table that no one but her could see. It reminded her of a photograph in the pub, and so she went over to check it out with her host. 'Yes, it looks like the girl,' she said.

The photograph was one of a set of three from the early 1900s found in the loft of the pub; it was presumed that they were earlier tenants. There was a married couple, another picture of a teenage boy and girl (him in Scout uniform) and the one of a child, who looked about three or four years old. Although the child wore a dress, boys of that age at that time were also put in a dress-like garment. We presumed that perhaps the child had died young and returned to haunt the place, and I told that story many times until I was contacted by a lady who had been researching her family, and had recognised a copy of the photo in the *Evening Star*.

Her information demonstrated just how a story can be innocently misinterpreted. She was of the Minter family, who owned a sweet shop at No. 5 Grimwade Street, which I had visited as a boy with my mother. Mum knew the family, who started out by the Dove in St Helen's Street, close to the Rope Walk where she started life. Valerie Robert's information was that the little girl was Laura Maud Francis (née Minter),

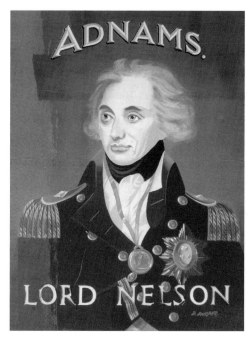

The Lord Nelson, Fore Street. *Photograph of a young child at the Lord Nelson.*

who was aged four in about 1894-5. She had grown up, and once ran the sweetshop in Grimwade Street. The teenage girl was Iris Newman, who carried on the shop until the 1980s. However, the Boy Scout, Willie, succumbed to consumption at the age of twenty. The older couple were Jack (Joseph) and Julia Minter (née Cutting), the parents of Laura. Jack was a cart builder who also made his friend Mr Zagni the first handcart for Peter's Ice Cream.

So how did those unrelated pictures hanging on the wall of the Lord Nelson come to be there? Well, it seems that the husband of Iris was estranged from her for forty years. When she died he immediately returned and had the house cleared by Osborne's, and much of her property was lost to the family and went to auction. Maybe a past landlord of the Lord Nelson bought the photos as part of a job lot with furniture, and, having no use for them, put them in the loft? Whatever happened, it seems unlikely that the ghostly child was Laura, who lived to a ripe age. It also leaves us with the question: 'if it was not Laura, then who was that visitor from the astral plane at the end of the table?'

The Weird Waggon at Isaac Lord

On the opposite side of Fore Street to the Lord Nelson is a beautiful medieval merchant house and warehouse (best seen from the dockside). Some timber from the oldest part of the building has been dated by dendrochronology to 1450. Cargo would have been stored in it from the docks and then transferred onto horse and cart for local delivery in the yard. The gates are often closed, but if they are open, take a look at that picturesque courtyard. The building is known by the name of the family firm that used to own it, Isaac Lord. There is an unusual but vivid apparition seen only occasionally when those gates are open. People have jumped away from the gates, seeing a horse and cart thundering towards them. It has no rider or load, so is quite unique amongst the more usual 'headless horseman and devilish carriage ghosts' one frequently encounters. Was there an accident there? Who knows? I spoke to one of the Lord family who was last to live there until about 2006. It had not appeared during his tenure, but who knows what may surprise the new owners – who have opened a bar and accommodation fronting onto No.7 Wherry Quay – at some time in the future?

Neptune Likes Sailors!

Further along Fore Street from Isaac Lords is the Old Neptune Inn, built in 1490, re-modelled in 1639 and closed in 1937. At one time it was an antiques shop and nowadays is a private house. I was once telling a party of people in the Lord Nelson that I had heard that there was supposed to be a sailor ghost there, but that was all I knew. As we were leaving, a lady customer on another table spoke to me, saying that she gathered I was the ghost tour guide. On confirming it, she informed me that she lived somewhere with a ghost.

'Where is that?' I asked, intrigued.

'The Neptune,' she replied, much to the amusement of the party.

'Isn't it a sailor?' I added, hoping for more information.

'It is not just any sailor,' she retorted indignantly. 'He is a sea captain, and he sat on my bed last week!'

The crowd probably thought it was a set-up scene with a paid stooge. It wasn't!

The Pool Hall Puzzle

Just beyond the Neptune, beside the new university buildings, an alleyway cuts through to the docks. At the end of it is a warehouse building used until recently as a pool hall. I visited there some time ago, having heard some garbled reports. The manager showed me a particular pool table. On being invited to go up to it, I felt a quite horrid sensation, as if something was looking over my shoulder, and the hair on my neck rose. I was asked if I could smell anything, but I had to deny that I could. The manager told me that some people were almost overcome by a stench at the table, whilst others a few feet away registered nothing. Floorboards had been raised in search of dead rats, but to no avail. By all accounts, many preferred not to play on it, saying it was 'unlucky'. Other employees added comments about unnatural noises emanating from upstairs after it had been locked, so who knows what lies in store for the next owner?

Isaac Lord, Fore Street.

The Old Neptune Inn and Neptune café.

The Salthouse Street Area

If you retrace your steps back past the Isaac Lord building to the Salthouse Street junction, you may notice a sloping drive opposite that leads to the old walled Jewish cemetery, on a 999-year lease (taken out in 1796). Jews were persecuted and driven out of England in 1290, and not allowed to return officially until 1656, when they were still subject to some legal restrictions. Some came to Ipswich, but there never seems to have been a large Jewish population, and the synagogue finally built in Rope Walk in 1792 was allowed to become derelict. It was demolished in 1877. It is known that in 1850 there were only five Jewish families in Ipswich, totalling twenty-three people.

After about 1850 Ipswich Jews started to use a graveyard in Colchester. A visitor has photographed small strange oscillating orbs of light, standing sentinel in front of the memorial stones, which are inscribed in fading Yiddish script.

Walk beyond the graveyard and you stumble across one end of the disused Green Man Lane, which ran from here back to the junction of Key Street and Salthouse Street, where the Green Man pub was situated on the corner of 55 Key Street, near to Salthouse Street and Slade Street.

The Jewish cemetery.

The Green Man

The Green Man (demolished long ago) is of interest in the story I was told by the burly dock workers of Pauls Mills in the 1970s. As I walked through the dock to work, they were already having their first tea break, having started very early to load lorries with sacks of flour that they hefted on their backs from the chutes. It was hard work and they often ended their lives with flour in their lungs, as nobody wore facemasks then. Every now and again one would spot a body floating in the dock, and would call his mates and the police. A couple of times the body of someone who had fallen in the dark was fished out. Most times, however, no body was found, despite drag nets and police divers. In those instances they blamed it upon William.

Apparently, William had been gambling on cards at the Green Man. After a good run of luck, another player accused him of cheating. Insulted, he left, and was not seen for a day or more. He turned up floating dead in the dock, with none of his winnings on him. Had the disgruntled loser followed him out, or had some other robber got lucky? If he had merely stumbled into the dock and drowned, surely the money would have been found on his body?

I have told the tale many times, but in one instance was talking to a women's club. Their leader rose to her feet at the end of the story, and they fell to a respectful silence. 'I do not know about the other stories this young man has told, but I can verify that last one,' she said. 'My husband was the police inspector in these parts, and many times he came home cursing "that damned William in the dock!"'

I have always found a lasting attraction for Green Man figures (faces with foliage growing out of mouths, ears or eyes) and frequently search them out in old Churches. Whilst I have not spotted any in Ipswich Churches, they can be found at the old Tolly Cobbold Brewery cottage on Cliff Quay, some Ipswich School library windows and above the door of Lloyds Bank on the Cornhill.

A Load of Old Bull?

As you come onto Key Street, the Old Bull Inn building, dating to the sixteenth century, is nearly opposite the back of the Customs House at No. 35, on the corner of Slade Street. A First World War German Zeppelin heading for the docks dropped a bomb on 31 March 1916 which hit the pub instead, and killed a man who lived next door to it. His ghost has been sighted from time to time. Alternatively, the spectre could be the wraith of Thomas Nichols. He was the landlord of the nearby Ram Inn, where a naval press gang congregated on 12 December 1778. They got into a fight with the dockers from the Green Man, and in the ensuing melee he was killed.

Now carefully cross the road to the Old Custom House, and go round the front onto the quayside. In my youth many graceful Thames sailing barges were moored there on Common Quay, including the *Cambria*, the last to be powered solely by sail. Its skipper, Bob Roberts, was supported by a director of Pauls millers, who ensured he had enough cargoes even if he took a bit longer to deliver them.

The Old Bull.

Thames Sailing Barge.

Unusual carving from the Old Bell Inn.

The Cranfields Mill Stones

Go towards Stoke Bridge past the impressive Old Custom House, built in 1845 on the site of an even older custom house (which had a bonded warehouse built into it, together with a small prison). The ducking stool now kept in Christchurch Mansion was once sited near here. The nearby firm of Cranfields was a rival miller to Pauls on Ipswich Dock. I was told of a mystery that happened around 1950 that has never been solved. The six massive paired sets of mill wheels needed replacing or redressing. They were at the top of the building, and were lifted out of their shafts by a dozen men using muscle power, chains and a block and tackle. Two stones were lowered onto a waiting lorry below to form part of a director's wall. The others were stashed around the outside of the room. As it was time to go home, the doors on each landing were locked. (They do this to prevent people from falling through the hatchways in the dark.)

The next day the door was unlocked again, and the millstones (as wide as 6-8ft, made of solid stone) were found scattered around like loose change. Even if a couple of jokers had crawled through the hatch, they would have been unable to lift the heavy objects by themselves. What happened has never successfully been explained.

Wringing Hands at the Old Bell

My uncle, Leslie Howe, was the landlord of the Old Bell Inn on the far side of Stoke Bridge from the dock. The pub was originally called the Seahorse, but changed its name to reflect some of its best customers – workers from a nearby bell foundry. The place reputedly dates from the early sixteenth century, and was originally the venue for cock fighting. It certainly had its share of 'things that go bump in the night' as well as a 'presence' in one particular bedroom; the presence manifests itself by causing the victim to feel a sudden and overpowering sensation of anxiety. A ghostly horseman was also credited with appearing in the yard. A carving on a corner post appears to be a hybrid of a cat's head and fish's tail. Could it be a catfish? It is likely to be the work of Mr Ringham, a famous nineteenth-century carver who is known to have done some work there.

The area name of 'Stoke' is thought to be derived from the Anglo-Saxon word for stockade, but the site possibly pre-dates the Anglo-Saxon era as a fortified hill amongst marshland. The medieval St Mary at Stoke Church on Stoke Street is possibly on the site of an even earlier wooden Church.

The Ransomes Tragedy

The area of Stoke was once synonymous with Ransomes & Rapier, a major employer in the town from 1869-1988. There were three businesses with Ransomes in the name, originating from the one set up by Quaker philanthropist Robert Ransome, who created an iron foundry in Old Foundry Road in 1789. He introduced a sick scheme for workers, and also gas-lamp lighting.

Although it was known principally for manufacturing agricultural machinery, its managing director in the early 1900s brought in a very different product to produce. Sir Wilfred Scott Stokes realised the danger of German machine-gun nests, and by December 1914 he demonstrated the prototype 3in Stokes Trench Mortar for dealing with them. (I think his Quaker predecessor would have been upset that his firm was now involved with ordnance.) They were seen as a low priority by officers who thought the war would soon be over, but the Americans saw the usefulness of having a mobile armament that could throw an 11-pound high-explosive bomb for 100 yards, and produced them under licence.

In the Second World War, the factory was the frequent target for bombing raids, as it produced armoured parts for the war effort. One self-priming bomb in the disguised shape of a tin can fell unexploded, and the man who tried to open it was killed – along with half a dozen workmates – by the resultant explosion. His un-named ghost was light-heartedly blamed for any accident or loss at the factory for years afterwards.

Someone more successful at defusing explosive devices was the Ipswich bomb-squad member who also designed the mock-Tudor 'Walk' and 'Thoroughfare' shopping precinct off Tavern Street. Major H.J. Leslie Barefoot (1887-1958) was awarded the George Cross for his efforts in the Blitz.

seven

GREAT PEOPLE

The Fate of Cardinal Wolsey

With your back towards Stoke Bridge, you can walk towards the town centre on Bridge Street and turn right into College Street by the redundant St Peter's Church (now an arts venue). It is reckoned that it was originally much closer to the dock in Saxon times, since the old waterfront was further behind where the modern quayside lies. The Church has a twelfth-century black Tournal marble font, one of only nine in England (and probably the finest). It is carved with lions. The Augustinian Monastery of St Peter and St Paul that adjoined it was suppressed to fund Wolsey's College next door. The plan was for the college to feed into a college he was founding in Oxford. That college was to be called Cardinal College, but with his demise it was named after Henry VIII. It was later renamed Christchurch College.

Beside St Peter's is the gateway to what was intended to be Wolsey's College, which was never completed – for Ipswich's most famous son fell from grace. Cardinal Thomas Wolsey was once thought to be a butcher's son (though this is now thought to be a later addition to his legacy designed to discredit him). His father, Robert Wolsey, was in fact a respected and wealthy cloth merchant married to one Joan Daundy. Robert died during the War of the Roses at the Battle of Bosworth Field (22 August 1485). They lived near St Nicholas' Church, Ipswich. Thomas Wolsey not only rose to be a cardinal, but also became the second most powerful man in the land when he was appointed chancellor to Henry VIII. When he failed to get his sovereign a divorce, however, his days were numbered. He had to give up Hampton Court Palace to the king, and he was about to be arrested for treason when he died of an illness in Leicester on 29 November 1530 at the age of sixty. Various people have claimed to have seen his ghost in Ipswich, but there are no substantive detailed reports.

If you turn left at another quayside Church, the fifteenth-century St Mary at the Quay, you will enter Foundation Street. Go across Star Lane and follow it until you see Smart Street on your right. Down there on the right, on the corner with Pleasant Row, is a disused college annexe, which is on the site of one of the Ragged Schools

Wolsey Gate, College Street.

Cardinal Wolsey going in procession to Westminster Hall by Sir John Gilbert PRWS.

of Ipswich. A teacher there once appeared to doze off in his chair in front of the class; the lads eventually realised that he had died. I can verify the tale, as my Uncle Cyril Howe was the caretaker at the time, and it was through him I came to know about the Ragged School and Alms Houses. The College Annexe was once a grammar school founded by Mr W. Smart. The library became a free facility for burgesses of the town in 1612. Behind it lay Pleasant Row and Shire Hall Yard, an ancient centre of local government. Head back onto Foundation Street and you cannot fail to miss the intriguing Tooley's Alms Houses.

Tooley's & Smart's Almshouses

Henry Tooley was a wealthy and important Tudor merchant, who started some almshouses in 1551 for ten poor widowers to live out their days in some degree of comfort, with preference given to men injured in defence of their country in the wars. Smart was a contemporary of similar position who did likewise. The buildings you see now are mainly Victorian rebuilding, around a pleasant central garden, and are used as a retirement home with a good atmosphere to this day.

The building has two separate ghosts: the first spectre is of a lady sitting sewing, seen upstairs in the central block. She is sewing a funeral shroud, and appears a couple of days before elderly residents die, thus giving the staff some warning. To explain about the second ghost I need to take you to the site of Blackfriars, further along the road on the same side.

Smart Street, the former site of almshouses and a Ragged School.

Tooley's Almshouses, Foundation Street.

The Pointing Black Friar

The ruins of the Blackfriars Dominican Friary of the Blessed Virgin can clearly be seen from Foundation Street. The outline of the massive St Mary's Church and its supporting pillars, and the friars' own chapter house, can clearly be seen. The narrow room seen alongside it would actually have descended below it, and be stocked with resonance jars to act as an echo chamber for their chants. In fact, the friary (founded around 1263) was the richest religious house in Ipswich, supported by the tithes of the many wealthy merchants living in that parish. The complex included a library and two hospitals (one exclusively for lepers) and covered an area from Star Lane and the defensive bank that originally ran along old Lower Brook Street (where indeed there was a brook, fed from the Spring Road area). Inevitably the Friary was closed during the Dissolution of the Monasteries in 1538.

We know much about the place thanks to a vicar's daughter called Nina Layard. She studied the buildings and all the documents connected with them for several years before publishing a comprehensive study paper about it in 1895. Naturally, the Ipswich Historical Society wanted it read at their meeting so they could discuss it. However, on the day it was read by a man (whilst Nina sat on a chair behind a curtain) since they did not allow lady members! I think it is a salutary lesson that no one remembers the name of that man. Anyway, she went on to make an important Anglo-Saxon archaeological dig at Boss Hall as well as several others (including the Foxhall Palaeolithic site), and ought to be much better remembered.

Inevitably there is evidence of the site's history in the form of a Black Friar ghost who is said to have a baleful glare and point or poke people, and to hover slightly above the ground. From this it is presumed that the ground level used to be higher than it is now.

*Blackfriars
Dominican Friary.*

But what about our other Tooley's Almshouse ghost? Let me elucidate. A man used to work at the nearby *East Anglian Daily Times* newspaper buildings. He used to walk to work, arriving at around 4.30 a.m., to collect a van full of newspapers for the local newsagents. They needed them early so that they could sort and mark them up for their paper-delivery boys. Because of the early start, he finished at lunchtime, and, as he walked home, would occasionally chat to the gardener outside Tooley's Almshouses. One such day, he asked if one of the elderly residents had been taken ill in the night. 'No, why do you ask?' was the reply. 'It was a quiet night. My wife the matron was on call, but was beside me in bed all night.' The man explained that on his way to work, earlier that morning, he had seen a figure in dark flowing clothes knocking on the door. Not getting a reply, he had walked to another door and entered. The gardener was disbelieving. 'That door has always been locked and hasn't been opened for years. I don't think we have even got a key.' They examined the door together, and witnessed the rust, cobwebs and weeds that confirmed the statement. It was only then that the newspaper employee wondered what he had really seen. In his experience, a figure in black, flowing clothes visiting at an unearthly hour of the morning was most likely to be a vicar coming to give last rites to the dying. He remained puzzled, and told his son about it (who in turn told me).

We know that wherever the Black Friars built their friaries, they kept to the same layout, and followed the same timed daily programme of work and prayers. From that it can easily be demonstrated that Tooley's Almshouses lie in the area the dormitories once stood. Remember that the place was closed down in 1538, and Tooley did not start construction until 1551. He may well have re-used some buildings, or, failing that, the stones (since they are a scarce commodity in Suffolk). It also strikes me that if your first prayers are before breakfast at 5 a.m., you might need someone to wake you up with a knock on the door of your cell (in the days before alarm clocks). I can also surmise that from a distance, in the dark, knocking can also look the same as poking or pointing. Was the mysterious 'clergyman' the same as the Black Friar from along the road? We may never know for sure, but it may make sense to you as it does me.

The Unicorn and Other Wild Beasts

The shadowed area in which you are in is often cool, even in summer, but in winter the wind can really shriek through. It is at that time of year that Suffolk storytellers will revive tales of the hideous hell-hound Black Shuck. (*Scucca* is the Anglo-Saxon word for a demon.) He is a huge, shaggy black dog with slavering mouth and red eyes the size of saucers, and also known by other names such as Galleytrot, Padfoot, Old Shug and Barguest. Look into those fiery eyes and you'll die, they reckon. He is in turn sometimes linked with the menacing Woden's Wild Hunt, a pack of haunting horsemen and malevolent creatures led in a chase by the Anglo-Saxon Lord of the Wild Winds, as they search for lost souls in the winter gales. One legendary creature can, however, be seen by everybody in this area, whatever the time of year: look up at the building that forms the corner of Foundation Street and No. 75 Orwell Place

The Catchpole Brewery and Unicorn pub.

(once known as Stepples Street). It has a tower surmounted by a unicorn weathervane on its nineteenth-century roof, and was the Catchpole brewery and Unicorn pub. The Catchpole brewery was registered there in 1918, and grew to have fifty-six pubs, but when it closed in 1923 they were divided between what, at that time, were two separate rival local breweries, Tollemache and Cobbold. They later merged. The Unicorn pub continued until 1976; after that was converted into a shop.

A carpet company took the lease, but only really used the ground floor, since there was no lift to transport heavy rolls of carpet between floors. Looking for an income for the basement, the manager agreed to rent it for a week or so to a lady wishing to put on a temporary art exhibition. She had not got quite enough of her own pictures to fill the space, so was also featuring works by two other artist friends. She was loaned a key so that she could visit in the evenings and weekend to set the exhibition up. It takes a lot of time to arrange the pictures so that the colours and sizes do not clash, and she was still working there on the Sunday before the Monday night opening. People had been invited with the lure of an exclusive preview and glass of wine, and a crowd duly assembled outside. When the place failed to open at the time specified on the invitations some started to drift away. Suddenly a man turned up, quite breathless. He apologised and explained that, unfortunately, the exhibition would not be opening that night. The crowd dispersed, and the next day the shop manager heard what had happened and was a bit mystified. The lady had paid the rent in advance, so there was no financial loss, but naturally he wondered what had occurred.

On the Wednesday a man appeared, saying that he had a letter of authorisation to remove all the artworks by the lady artist. He had been the same chap who had broken the news on the Monday night, and was one of the other two artists being exhibited. He said that late on Monday he had a phone call from his friend, saying that the exhibition was incomplete, and that many of the pictures were not yet hung on the wall. She said that she had run out of the building on the Sunday morning, scared for her life, and had vowed never to return – and what's more, she was even refusing to leave her own home at present. She would not discuss what had happened, but she was still extremely frightened. I would love to know some further details, but that is all I have ever been able to find out. Two people I know who have a more recent connection to the building (currently a charity shop) have no complaints.

Thomas Gainsborough and the Rocking Chair Ghost

Return back down Foundation Street on the opposite side, past the multi-storey car park. Just the other side of Rosemary Lane is an office building (No. 32) and a vacant lot. The vacant lot is where the house of a more famous artist, Thomas Gainsborough, once stood. He moved there from Sudbury to paint wealthy residents, then on to Bath (where he gained the patronage of the high society that met there to 'take the waters').

The office building next door, overlooking Tooley's Almshouses, opposite, has had many occupants, but none stranger than the one in the basement. It has been a union office, architects and mental-health centre in recent years, but the original occupants are a mystery.

A married couple were employed to clean the building each evening. One night the lady went down into the basement (which, if you are tall enough to see over the wall, can be seen from Rosemary Lane that runs alongside it). She had gone to fetch more cleaning materials, but came back in a hurry with a description of something quite different: the wraith of a man in a peaked cap, smoking a pipe in a rocking chair. 'Have you ever seen him?' she asked.

'Oh yes, but I didn't want to scare you, dear,' was her husband's sanguine reply. (Notice how he still let her go down there alone though!) They compared notes and agreed descriptions. They also agreed that he looked a nice old man, and seemed oblivious to their presence, so was unlikely to harm them. They continued working there for a month or two more and saw him again several times. They still continued to go to the basement alone, not seeing any reason to be scared. They enquired with their employers, but his identity was not known.

Whilst I have seen some dubious internet videos of empty rocking chairs moving by themselves, I must confess that I was rather pleased to have this tale to tell, and impressed upon people it was the only rocking-chair ghost I had ever come across. One fateful night a couple in the crowd replied that they had stayed at a guest house in Cromer on the Norfolk coast with a rocking-chair ghost. Quick as a flash, one of my other customers quipped, 'Ah, that's just him gone on a holiday!'

Incidentally, further down Foundation Street is the Masters House, originally home to William King, a pioneer of the Co-operative movement in the eighteenth century.

Old Winter the Wizard

If you turn from Foundation Street into Rosemary Lane, the adjacent multi-storey car park on your right looks an ugly site. It covers a once derelict area that bore witness to

No. 32 Foundation Street.

a character from long ago. When I was young, in the 1950s, it was a crowded network of streets, too narrow to get a car down. There was Little Wingfield Street (between numbers 8/10 Foundation Street) and Wingfield Street (between numbers 24/26.) In fact, at one point you could shake hands across the path between one bedroom window and its opposite number, as the houses that bore them leant together like a conspiracy of friends. The area was demolished in 1962, and was named after Sir Anthony Wingfield KG (1485-1552), who acted as executor to King Henry VIII.

There are a couple of references to a man known as Old Winter in Ipswich Library. There is one other mention of him, which I believe to be a later fabrication, attached to the Angel Lane story (Old Winter allegedly told a farmer how to get rid of Mrs Pett, the woman who spontaneously combusted in Ipswich). One of the references put him living in 1795, and both credit him with being a wizard or cunning man. It was common in those days for every area to have a cunning man, wise woman or the like practicing folk medicine or brewing love spells. Most were pretty harmless, and avoided being noticed by the gentry as they served the poorer part of the community. Old Winter seemed to have come to their notice because of his sense of natural justice.

One night he was walking out late when he spied a thief crouched in a garden plot, stealing vegetables. He pointed at the man and walked off. The thief was stuck there all night, unable to move, cramped, cold, wet and terrified. As people moved about the next morning they spotted him, and soon surmised who had been purloining their produce. Old Winter returned, waved his hand, and the man was able to leave. The reputation of Old Winter grew.

A farmer from the edge of town, hearing of his reputation, came to ask for help. (He probably gave him the traditional Suffolk farmers greeting: 'I'm a poor farmer!' still used to this day.) He explained that his barn had blown down. He was trying to replace it, but expensive materials had gone missing from the place. 'I'll keep watch tonight, to see what happens,' vowed the cunning man. The farmer offered to keep him company, and said he knew a place they could hide. Later that night the back door to a farm worker's cottage opened, and a man stepped quietly into the moonlight, across the field and stile until he came to where the construction materials were stored. Hefting a large beam of seasoned timber across his shoulder, he made his way back across the field. By the time Old Winter and the farmer had emerged from their hiding place the thief was half way home. Once more Old Winter pointed.

Suddenly the man was confused. Despite living in the area he couldn't find the route back to his cottage or the stile. What is more, the stolen timber started to weigh heavier and heavier on his shoulder, and seemed stuck fast there. He was still staggering around in blind panic when the pair caught up with him. Old Winter waved his hand once more, and there was the farmer, his face looming angrily from a hand's breadth away. 'I gave you a job and a place to live, and this is how you paid me back!' he muttered angrily. Snatching the now-light timber from the man's shoulder, he snarled, 'You're sacked, and out of that house in the morning!' (No industrial tribunals in those days!)

Inevitably, respect for Old Winter's reputation grew even more. As I said, that happened in the late 1700s, over 200 years ago. Yet when I frequented the area as a youngster I would sometimes hear mothers use his name as a bogey man, e.g. 'Come in for tea now, or Old Winter will have you.'

eight

UPPER BROOK STREET AND OLD CATTLE MARKET

Two Styles of Management

Carry on walking to the end of Rosemary Lane. If you look from the end of it across Lower Brook Street, there is an old building (No. 16) used as offices on the corner of Turret Lane (named after a now demolished house which had a turret). To the right its neighbour, No. 14, is a youth centre. The stories behind those buildings demonstrate two very different styles of management, especially when it came to dealing with the supernatural.

A retired electrician told me how every year or so he was asked to call at the youth-centre building, which in those days was an office. It had male manager and half a dozen middle-aged ladies working there. He would be asked to take a look at an old electric heater in the corner. After making sure it was switched off he would remove the lid and rattle a screwdriver about, but not really perform any constructive maintenance or repair. After putting it back together, he was thanked and the bill would subsequently paid. Of course there was nothing wrong with it – it was all a charade set up by the manager to keep his staff happy. Every now and again someone would see a shimmering in the corner and he would blame the heater and summon the electrician, rather than admit to the rather indistinct disembodied soul that manifested there. His style was to keep the workers in blissful ignorance, rather than risk them getting scared.

The large bustling office on the corner was a very different kettle of fish. The manager was barely thirty, and his staff all younger, so it was a lively place to work. The company thrived and expanded, and have since moved to larger premises to cope with the growth. Maybe the straightforward attitude of their manager was partly responsible for that. One of his young female staff told me what happened one afternoon.

The manager walked into the front office and as bold as brass exclaimed, 'I think I have just seen a ghost!' Naturally the staff were interested to hear the details. As he was

Nos 14-16 Foundation Street.

coming down the stairs, he said, a figure of a woman came up towards him, dressed all in white, with a white headdress 'like some old-fashioned nurse'. She had passed through his arm whilst ascending, then disappeared. The staff did not appear to be fazed by this, and some thought it was quite 'cool' to work in a haunted building, and hoped they would see it too. The manager had obviously judged the nature of his staff well, and trusted them to deal with his matter-of-fact description.

I did some research and found, to my surprise, that the building was known as one of the 'old hospital houses' of Ipswich. Most of them are nearer the docks area, but obviously this one is a little further out. In the days when Royal Naval ships frequently visited the port of Ipswich, they sometimes had casualties aboard. Richer officers may have been returned to their families or private hospitals to nurse, but there was very little provision for the lower ranks of sailors and marines wounded in defence of their country. Some charitable locals were urged to take some in, and looked after them. With few trained nurses, it would have been down to the wives and daughters of households to take on that role.

The most common injury was splinters: not the annoying little splinters that stick in your fingers, but great sharp spears of wood smashed from wooden ships by cannonballs. Apparently there were also a couple of doctors who gave their services for free – or for expenses only – who also could have advised on treatments. I discovered that there were at least two houses that took in wounded prisoners of war – a supreme act of kindness at a time when we had been at war for more than a century with the French, Dutch or Spanish. Imagine being asked nowadays to put up a couple of wounded enemies in your spare bedroom. (A cynic once asked if, once recovered, they were taken out and shot... In fact they were usually transferred to prisoner-of-war camps where they were eventually swapped for British prisoners of war.)

So it was not altogether surprising that the manager saw a nurse-like ghost. She was probably a member of the kind household who lived there, and I think the existence

An early nurse in uniform.

of the hospital houses says something very complimentary about the people of Ipswich at that time.

The Mirror-Cracker Ghost

Turn down Turret Lane. A hollowed-out tree trunk lining a well here was found to date back to AD 670. At the end of the lane you will come out on what used to be the Old Cattle Market of Ipswich, which was moved in 1856 to Portman Road. On the other side of the bus station that now occupies this space you will see the Plough Inn, on the corner of Dog's Head Street. The name of the street refers to an older pub (created by incoming seventeenth-century Flemish migrants) called 'The Dog's Head in a Pot', shown on a 1674 map as standing on the north-east corner of the lane (where Sainsbury's is now situated). The Flemish dialect still has the term in its colloquial sayings: it means 'a slovenly household'. The pub sign would have been a dog

The Plough Inn,
Old Cattle Market.

licking out a cooking pot. In other words, the house did not bother with washing up! But I digress – let's get back into the Plough, where I sometimes worked as a DJ in the early 1970s.

The pub was run by a Yorkshire couple, Jim and Doris Biddulph. Jim was known as 'Ban 'Em Biddulph' on account of his frequent action, but he usually let people have a second chance. His wife suggested that he convert an old junk-filled box room into a spare bedroom so that they could offer a room to any of their relatives visiting the area from Yorkshire. Jim set to and cleaned, painted and wallpapered. He got a bed and wardrobe, and as a finishing touch decided to attach a mirror to the wall. Carefully drilling and raw-plugging the wall, he attached the mirror. However, he later found that it had cracked across one corner. Disappointed, he purchased another mirror of the same model. After checking for flaws he screwed it to the wall using the same attachment points, but made sure he did not over-tighten the screws in case the mirror bent against the wall. A couple of days later he found it smashed on the floor. Giving up on that style of mirror, but wanting to cover the screw holes in his new decoration, Jim obtained a large mirror (with a stout chain and a hook to hang it from the picture rail). Within a week or so the chain had snapped, hurling the mirror on the floor to shatter. Curiously, the link of the chain had broken near the middle, as if it had been pulled apart by a great force. We reminded him that the seven years' bad luck for each broken mirror were stacking up, and was it his face that was causing it? He was not amused, and bought a free-standing mirror for use on the dressing table. It too ended up on the floor, broken. He laughed it off as an unseen 'mirror-cracker ghost.'

I have retold the tale many times since the mid-seventies, but one night was interrupted by an electrician, who said he could bet which room it was. 'Have you heard this story before?' I asked. 'No,' he replied, 'but that is what makes it so interesting. Is it the small room in the middle upstairs, at the rear of the wing facing the bus station?' he asked. I confirmed it was, and asked him how he knew.

'I did not know about the mirrors,' he explained, 'but my firm has rewired the light in that room three times. Light bulbs are always going out in there.'

A few months later a female manager took over the pub, and my friend Ed and I got to know her as we often had a drink there before or after a ghost tour. One night I asked her about the room, and she said that it now had an old desk and filing cabinet in it, but was not used much because of its small size. We told her the story, as she did not know it. A few months later we ran our last ghost tour before Christmas, and called in for a drink. On leaving I wished her a merry Christmas. 'It will be a special Christmas for me,' she said smiling. 'My boyfriend is giving up the sea and moving in. It will be our first Christmas together.' Returning in January, I was greeted with 'you and your blinking ghosts!' (We often get the blame just for re-telling the stories.) She explained that she had never told her boyfriend about our ghost story in her letters to him. When he had arrived just before Christmas, he was laden with bags and boxes to move in. Going upstairs to the living quarters he asked where he should dump his stuff. She had indicated the old box room. The door was ajar when he entered, but with his hands full he had pushed the light switch on using his elbow. The bulb lit briefly, but then went out. Leaning out of the door to inform her, to his horror he saw a shadowy figure slink along the passageway and then disappear.

In his rising terror he wondered if had he had done the right thing by moving in. Happily, however, he decided to stay, and the result was that about a year later a baby was born. As he grew, he would frequently crawl with toys from one end of the long upstairs corridor to the other, between his own room and the living room, passing the box room on the way. The door was generally ajar as it did not close easily, and the youngster ventured inside. However, when words started at around two years old, the names 'mum' and 'dad' were followed by 'nasty man' as he was carried past the room. He had never had the tale told in front of him.

nine

SILENT STREET, ST NICHOLAS STREET AND ST PETER'S STREET

The Silent Street

You can take the narrow lane than runs from Old Cattle Market between the buildings to Silent Street. It was originally called Half Moon Street after a local pub, and was adjacent to the descriptively named Cold Dung Hill, but its own revised name reminds us of a time of death and disease. The poor tenement blocks were denuded of their residents (often families of ten living in a single room without sanitation) by an outbreak of a smallpox epidemic, and it thus got a name of macabre origin. Plague pits have been discovered nearby, filled with poor souls buried together without much order. Ipswich has always been susceptible to plagues because of its role as an important port, and Black Death, Leprosy, Dysentery, Cholera, all claimed large numbers of citizens in the years before adequate hygiene, medicine, sanitation and drainage were introduced.

Turn left onto Silent Street and you will notice a fine antiquarian bookshop, Claude Cox, on your right. Books reputedly move from their ordered shelves overnight to appear in inappropriate sections. Walk past it and you will meet with the junction of St Nicholas Street and St Peter's Street, where there is an unusual octagonal Victorian postbox. Curzon House once stood on the left-hand (south-east) corner. It was used as a hospital for sailors injured in the war with the Dutch, and straw was placed on the road to deaden the noise of passing wagons. Lord Curzon, who died in 1535, was visited there by King Henry VIII and his queen of the time, Catherine of Aragon. Curzon had attended King Henry at the magnificent 'Field of the Cloth of Gold' meeting. The house was later used as the Elephant & Castle pub.

Bar IV in St Peter's Street was known to have plenty of ectoplasm to spare, in the form of the ghosts of a girl, a monk and a cat in its cellar (seen in the days when it was known as the Toad & Raspberry, and then The Blackadder).

Silent Street.

The Hippodrome, St Nicholas Street.

Child star Shirley Temple.

On the opposite side of St Nicholas Street from Silent Street once stood the top music hall in Ipswich, the Hippodrome Variety Theatre, converted later into the Savoy Ballroom and Bingo Hall. Cardinal House was built over its site. The Bostock family owned both the Hippodrome (which opened 27 March 1905) and the Lyceum theatre in Carr Street. Bostock, an ex-circus proprietor, owned many theatres, and was adept at using publicity stunts to advertise his business. On the opening of the Hippodrome he lured Madame Florence from a rival business in Woodbridge Road to walk on a giant globe to the theatre, where he also featured a group of performing elephants.

The theatre apparently once had the blood-curdling sight of the ghost of an old musician who used to be seen around what was the orchestra pit. He had got so drunk one night after a show that he fell in the road and was hit by a horse and carriage. The music hall competed successfully against other halls in Tower Street and Bramford Road for many years, bringing in top acts such as Harry Champion (known for hits such as 'Henry VIII', 'Any Old Iron' and 'Boiled Beef & Carrots') and Shirley Temple. My dad fetched fish and chips for Harry and carried the young Miss Temple's bags – what a claim to fame. Other famous acts appeared: they included Gus Elen, Wilson, Keppler & Betty, Marie Lloyd, George Formby, Sandy Powell, Max Miller and Arthur English.

The theatrical history of Ipswich is a fine one: it is believed that William Shakespeare performed with the Admiral's Men at the Griffin Inn on Westgate Street between AD 1580 and 1590. It later became the Crown & Anchor Hotel, but is now WH Smith's.

David Garrick, the most famous actor of his generation, made his stage debut in 1741 at the Playhouse. The theatre was built in 1736 in Tacket Street (at the time known as Tankard Street). Garrick went on to become a star in London and elsewhere.

The Ipswich Arts Theatre in Tower Street and its successor, the Wolsey Theatre, Civic Drive continue a fine theatrical tradition in the town.

The Gentlemanly Ghost

One night Tommo (who we met before at the Purple Shop) took his wife out to the Galleys restaurant (on your right at No. 25 St Nicholas Street). He left the table to go to the upstairs loo. As he approached the door, the latch handle moved, and the door opened. He flattened himself against the narrow stairwell wall to allow whoever was exiting space to get past, but no one appeared. He entered, and found nobody inside. On exiting, the door opened for him again. Somewhat shaken, he told the manager downstairs that 'something odd' had just happened to him. 'That will be our gentlemanly ghost,' replied the manager. Some staff had actually seen a shadowy figure from the corner of the eye but grown used to him. Next door, at Butts Wine Bar (now called Keos), there seems to be a similar guest upstairs.

The opposite side of the road is where Cardinal Wolsey's parents lived, backing onto the Churchyard of St Nicholas' Church. If you make a diversion to it via Cromwell Square you can see an unusual tomb outside. A skeleton is rising from its coffin and pointing to the page of a book with an arrow, as if to say 'You're next!' St Nicholas' Church has a carving of a saint (George or Michael?) killing a dragon in it, and was next to the Franciscan Greyfriars (founded in 1298 and giving its name to the areas

Galleys Restaurant, St Nicholas Street.

Statue of the Russian Prince Alexander Obolensky.

of Franciscan Way and Greyfriars). Some masonry from the building of the friary is incorporated into the wall of Saxon House office on the corner of Cromwell Square.

The Russian Prince

Opposite Galleys is a modern statue of the Russian Prince Alexander Obolensky. He was brought to England as an infant for safety by his mother during the Russian Revolution of 1917. He became a naturalised Englishman and excelled at rugby, helping England to win for the first time against New Zealand All Blacks at Twickenham in 1936. He scored two remarkable tries on his debut match, a feat which won him the nickname 'Prince of Pace'. He joined the RAF in the Second World War and died at the young age of twenty-four when his Hurricane fighter crashed at Martlesham in 1940. No doubt his inspiring spirit joined the many that haunt that base today.

Spooks

Going past Cromwell Square you will see on your left, at Numbers 10-12 St Nicholas Street, the Orissa restaurant, which was originally called Spooks, and had a supernatural theme of ghosts, skeletons, tombstones etc. The reason it was themed that way is because it was already known to be haunted before the restaurant was created. The disembodied top half of a lady known as Sylvia haunted downstairs and seemed to jam the door of the ladies loo at times. She was seen by our assistant Judi Yeatman one night when we took a party there.

Orissa restaurant,
formerly Spooks,
St Nicholas Street.

Upstairs the ghost of an unhappy dwarf who hanged himself there is said to haunt and cause mishaps, particularly around one particular table: if a bill was wrong or an order incorrect it always seemed to be on that table. One night a waitress brought a tray with two drinks on for a couple sitting there. Now I have seen mishaps where a tray has been allowed to tip drinks off one end, but what happened then was quite different: the two drinks left the tray from opposite sides and hovered momentarily before crashing to the ground. The startled couple had their bill paid for them.

Early one afternoon two of the staff were laying up tables ready for the evening. One whispered to the other one, 'Look at the table'. A fork was slowly revolving around on the bare wooden table by itself. One of the girls refused to work upstairs any longer, and instead managed the downstairs bar.

Weird Happenings at Wedding World

I once went out with a lovely lady called Gill who owned the Anglian Wedding World at No. 4 St Nicholas Street. The eighteenth-century shop stood next but one to the corner of St Nicholas Street and Friars Street. Originally she displayed goods downstairs and had a curtained fitting room upstairs, but so many brides-to-be and their mums complained of the 'cold, bad feeling' they felt up there that she decided to change things around. When I got to know her the changing room had just been moved downstairs, leaving ugly holes in the wall upstairs where the curtain rail used to be attached. Hoping to please her, I offered to fill in the holes and paint over them.

When I arrived at the shop one morning she was just leaving for the bank, but said her assistant would be there to make me a cup of tea later. I started work upstairs but

Former Anglian Wedding World shop, No. 4 St Nicholas Street.

was overcome with a funereal, creeping feeling of dread. Finally it got so uncomfortable to be there that I went downstairs to ask for a warming cup of tea. The assistant took one look at me and said, 'So you feel it too?' It was only then that I learnt the reason why the changing room had been shifted. I did go back upstairs to finish the job, but must admit I did it as quickly as possible.

Whilst you are in the area you may want to nip around the corner into Friars Street to see the unique Unitarian Meeting House, built in 1699 with a timber frame and cobweb windows. It has a marvellous octagonal high pulpit and box pews, and a spy hole in the door, originally inserted to look out for the enemies of Non-Conformists who would try to disrupt services.

ten

THE CORNHILL AND LLOYDS AVENUE

From St Nicholas Street proceed up Queen Street to its junction with Buttermarket and King Street. To your right you may spot the statue of 'Grandma Giles' looking up to the window where her famous *Daily Express* cartoonist creator Carl Giles (1916-95) worked. (He was called Ronald at his birth in Angel Islington, but cruel friends later compared his look to Boris Karloff, later shortened to Carl.) Turn left into King Street, and the Swan Inn is on your left.

Murder at the Swan

The Times of 14 March 2006 gave details of a murder that happened there from long ago, and its ongoing consequences for the owners today:

> A PUB must pay a fine for a murder on its premises more than 300 years ago. Auditors discovered the long-forgotten penalty for The Swan in Ipswich, Suffolk, while balancing the books for the town's St Mary Le Tower Church Charities. The annual bill of 40 shillings, equivalent to £2, seems to be a punishment for a killing in 1664 when Charles II was king.
>
> Rowell Bell is the clerk to trustees for a number of small charities, including Parker Gift 1664. He found the fine in a book called *An Account of the Gifts and Legacies that have been given and bequeathed to Charitable Uses in the Town of Ipswich — with some account of the present state and management and some proposals for the future regulation of them*. It reads: 'Mr. J. Parker to give 40 shillings a year to be paid out of The Swan Inn of this parish to buy coals for the poor (to be distributed on St Thomas's Day).' The gift is alleged to be for a perpetual fine imposed in 1664 consequent upon a murder committed at The Swan.

Forty shillings was a huge amount of money in 1664 — a labourer would have to work for six months to earn it. Mr Bell said:

> The money should be given to the trustees and although they won't still be buying coal, they will use their common sense. I expect, for example, they will pay for poor people to have bed

and breakfast or give it to charities which help the homeless. I think some people will be confused because The Swan has 1707 on it, and this dates back to 1664. But 1707 is probably the date refurbishment work was done.

Simon Trenter and Pam Wilson, who run The Swan, have agreed to pay the fine, which includes backdated payments to 1999, when the bill was last paid. Ms Wilson said: 'We are all intrigued. We like being part of history.'

Maybe this is connected to a story I heard from an old friend. He works from teatime until late at night, then goes home and sleeps until midday. Living by himself, he sometimes wanders the town in the afternoon, calling in at various pubs on the way. (However, this should not colour your opinion as to the veracity of his story!) He told me that one afternoon he decided to call into the Swan and, on his way in, saw a man sitting at one of the windows. When he got inside the man was gone, and the only occupant was the barman. 'If it weren't for me and that other chap, you'd have nothing to do at all,' he laughed.

'What other chap?' asked the barman. 'You are the first person in here in an hour – disturbing my afternoon read of the newspaper.' Until then my friend had presumed the other man had gone out back to the toilet, but he now asked more questions. The barman insisted there had not been anyone sitting at the window for at least an hour. A week or two later my friend experienced the same thing again, but it has not re-occurred since, and I have never been told the tale by anyone else.

The Corn Exchange Corpses

The Corn Exchange was built in 1878 but converted into an entertainment venue in 1975. Part of it is built upon the site of St Mildred's Church, which extended through to the Cornhill. It may explain the ghostly monk seen at the back of the basement film theatre on more than one occasion. The spirit of a small child has been encountered too, and during alterations a child's grave was discovered, probably missed when the Churchyard was cleared. The phantom that interests me though is of a more recent vintage, and his name is Jack.

I first encountered Jack in the 1970s when I disc jockeyed at massive Monday night discotheques at the Corn Exchange. It was quite a squeeze getting the large loudspeakers and other gear in or out, but Jack always helped us by holding doors and the lift, and always took an interest in what I did. He was very untypical of the 'jobsworth' sort of staff I met at many other halls. He was popular with the other staff and customers too, and would greet everyone personally at the front of house, and bid them farewell and a safe journey at the end of the evening. He had a prodigious memory for names, and addressed hundreds of people by theirs without ever a mistake. Long after I finished working at the disco I continued to see him at live shows I attended. After many years of service he came up for retirement, but as he did not want to go he continued to be employed on a casual basis when shows were on. He was a bachelor, and regarded himself as part of the entertainment business.

I later met a lady who worked on the box office and who told me what happened next. One night, after the show had ended and the audience gone home, the staff were locking up and realised that Jack was missing. He was found dead in the chair in the room where he put on his outdoor shoes and coat. Whilst everyone was sad, they agreed it was probably exactly the way he would have wanted to have gone. As the lady explained, though, he was not altogether gone: 'He is still around in the place he loved,' she said, 'And I for one don't mind.' During his time employed at the Corn Exchange he was known for his harmless jokes and tricks. It seemed he carried them on after death. One would happen whenever she got out a reel of tickets to replace a roll in the machine: when she turned round she would find they had gone, to turn up on the shelf behind her (where he had placed them on his way past).

There was another jape he played too: often the lady would be working alone in the box office and have to wait for the queue to disappear before she could go off to the loo. Returning (often in a hurry and finding another queue formed) she would sit straight down onto her stool, and find her nose level with the counter. Jack had been by and given it a whirl to decrease the height whilst she was gone. It continued after he was supposed to be gone, and the rest of the staff insisted it was not them continuing the joke.

The Ghoulish Golden Lion

Carry on past the Corn Exchange entrance and turn right into the lane known as Lion Street (which was originally St Mildreds Lane). You will pass the sixteenth-century Golden Lion Inn as you enter the Corn Hill Square. A man once met his mistress there, and she urged him to leave his wife for her. He refused, and she threatened to tell her of the affair. To prevent this he strangled her in the room, and was later caught and hanged. The room is colder than the rest, and still used as a guest room. One night my colleague Ed had a party of people enthralled with the tale on the stairs. When he tried to open the door it resisted, and he presumed that the staff had forgotten to unlock it for them. Telling the crowd he would have to squeeze past them back to reception for the key, his hand was suddenly pulled by the handle and he staggered into the room. The door had opened by itself! The crowd were convinced that it was a trick, but as he told me later it wasn't. Many people say that they would like to see something really spooky on a ghost tour, but do not recognise it when occasionally it happens!

A few years ago a flattened and mummified cat was found in foundations during building work. It is now kept in a box behind the bar, since the owner was persuaded that it was bad luck to dispose of it: they are meant to keep evil spirits away.

Golden Lion Hotel, Cornhill.

Burnt at the Stake

The area now taken up by the frontage of the Town Hall (built in 1868) once consisted of two taverns (the Sickle and the Kings Head, demolished in 1882) and the Guild Hall of Corpus Christi, St Mildred's Church. The Court of Common Pleas was later created in part of the old St Mildred's buildings, and the Bell Inn stood to the right of the Town Hall. The court existed on the Cornhill from the end of the Anglo-Saxon Thingstead era (*see* Packhorse Inn) until its removal to St Helen's Street in about 1786. There is in existence one of the oaths sworn by Portmen of Ipswich, who were some of the court officers:

> Portman's oath, mid-fifteenth century.
> You shall swear to well and faithfully keep and govern the town of Ipswich and maintain, to the best of your ability, all liberties, franchises and good customs of the town. And to give your full aid and support to the indifferent rendering of judgements of the court, with equal regard to every person, both rich and poor. And do the best you can for the honour of the town, so help you God.

One of the people tried at that court was Alice Driver. She had been apprehended in 1558 by a mob after she was caught hiding in a haystack with a weaver called Alexander Gooch at Grundisburgh. (She had previously hidden him in the house that she shared with her husband, Edward.) They were accused of heresy (i.e. holding different beliefs from the Catholic majority). Not attending Church regularly was proof enough of subversion, but Alice had obtained a prohibited English edition of the Bible and had been reading it, sufficient cause for Justice Noone to pursue her and Alexander. They were first detained at Melton prison, near Woodbridge, and then sent for trial at Bury St Edmunds Assizes in front of Sir Clement Heigham, MP for Ipswich and Speaker of the House of Commons. He had been involved in the trial and execution of two other Ipswich Protestant martyrs, Agnes Potten and Joan Trunchenfield, in 1556; Joan had assisted the Presbyterian minister Robert Samuel, burnt in 1555.

Seeking to trick Alice, they asked why she did not attend Church regularly. She replied that though she was happy for others to do so, she was a Protestant, and believed in worshipping a different way. 'But if the Catholic Church is good enough for royalty, why not for you?' In her reply she accused the Catholic Queen Mary of being 'a Jezebel'. (She was reputed to wear make-up on her face, a sin according to Protestants!) For that, Heigham ordered that both her ears be cut off, and sent the pair back for Inquisition at Ipswich by Dr Spenser, the Chancellor of Norwich, after another stay at Melton. No lawyer would defend Alice because if she was found guilty (and accused heretics were usually found guilty) all her property would be forfeit to the state and Church, leaving nothing for a legal fee. Any lawyer acting without the possibility of gaining a fee would be regarded suspiciously. So Alice defended herself.

She must have been an educated woman: she argued law with the lawyers and scripture with the clerics. Churchmen were frequently employed by courts because they were able to read and write. For every biblical text they quoted at her she replied with whole sections of scripture learnt by heart. Nonetheless, the pair were found guilty and sentenced to be burned at the stake on the Cornhill, outside the court. A large crowd gathered by the Octagonal Market Cross that used to stand in the square. (It was surmounted by a large goddess figure that now lives inside the Town Hall.) Many of the crowd were supporters of the outspoken martyr. In those days it was unusual for the last words of people to be noted, but in her case an exception was made. People sometimes talk blithely about being tied to the stake. In reality, ropes would have burnt through, permitting the victim to escape, so three chains were used instead: one at the feet, waist and neck. When they attached the neck chain, and as she was about to be cruelly burnt alive, she was heard to say, 'Oh! Here is a goodly neckerchief; blessed be God for it.' In other words – I will still believe what I want!

Alice Driver and Alexander Gooch were executed on 4 November 1558, just two weeks before Queen Mary died and the Protestant Queen Elisabeth I took over. If their trials had been a little later there is a chance that they may have been pardoned by the new royal administration. Their names are recorded, alone with those of seven other Protestant martyrs who had suffered similarly hideous executions, on a stone memorial in Christchurch Park. Their ghosts are still said to haunt the Cornhill, but it is many years since I have heard a modern report of it, and sadly few local people

Monument to nine Protestant martyrs, Christchurch Park.

seem to know their tragic story. Not every martyr was recorded as such at the time: Thomas Bilney had been seized from the pulpit of St George's Church near Westgate for preaching Reformation, and was eventually burnt in Norwich. Ann Bolton and John and Michael Trunchenfielde were burnt in Ipswich, but Agnes Wardal escaped. Other local people recorded on the memorial are N. Peke (1538), Kerby (1546) Revd Robert Samuel (1555), all whom were burnt in Ipswich in the years shown. John Tudson was burnt in London (1556) and William Pikes (1558) was burnt in Brentford.

Of course within a century it was time for the Protestants to start persecuting the few Catholics left in Ipswich (including the Sparrowe family of the Ancient House), but no memorial exists for them.

Those who were hanged in the eighteenth century were often also donated by the courts for medical dissection as a part of their punishment. For example, the *Ipswich Journal* of 2 April 1785 reported that John Wilkinson and his wife Ellen were executed at Rushmere, Ipswich for the murder of Martha Wilkinson, their youngest daughter; after the hanging, Wilkinson's body was delivered to Mr Bucke of Ipswich and his wife to Mr Abbot of Needham for dissection.

Other features of the Cornhill included a Rotunda in the south-east corner, which replaced the 'Shambles', an area of butchers' stalls. It was topped with a statue of the goddess Ceres, who after a few identity changes ended up inside the Town Hall, to the left of the main entrance, where she can still be seen. The Shambles had a stout post for attaching bulls to, so that they could be 'baited' by dogs before slaughter (something thought essential at the time for the quality of the meat).

Other punishments practiced on the Cornhill include at least two pressings to death (*peine forte et dure*) in 1519. Prisoners who refused to enter a plea in court in the sixteenth–eighteenth centuries were sometimes pressed to death by weights if they continued not to plead. Some minor offenders were tied to the back of a cart and whipped as it moved around the square three circuits. The stocks were also erected on the space in around 1607, where miscreants would have rubbish thrown at them whilst confined to a wooden frame.

Dastardly Doings in Debenhams

Whilst still at school in the late 1960s I had a Saturday job at Footman's department store; it eventually became Debenhams, and can still be seen on the opposite side of the Cornhill. There was a coffee shop there, but I did not have much to do with it as I worked in the food hall.

Years later I bumped into its retired manager, who told me what had gone on there at the time (although the staff were kept in the dark). It was decided to revamp Springles Coffee Shop. A firm of shop fitters were contracted to do the job as quickly as possible so as to minimise lost sales. They were due to arrive on Saturday as the place closed and work through the night. The store was closed on Sundays and Mondays in those days, so it gave them the maximum run of time without being in the way of customers. On the Sunday morning the store general manager popped by to see how they were doing. To his dismay, none of the tradesmen were working. They stood around outside of the café area looking a bit sheepish. 'What is going on?' he demanded. 'Why aren't you getting the job finished?' One of the workmen exclaimed, 'I am not going back in there!'

The men described how a woman with a hideously contorted face had driven them out. They were used to working in the dark and at night in empty buildings, but this frightful fiend was more than they were prepared to put up with. Their manager was called, but was unable to persuade them. He noticed that some were so frightened that they had abandoned valuable tools where they had been dropped, most unusual for a profession usually very protective of equipment being taken by other contractors from different areas. Eventually, the contract was re-let to another shop-fitting company, and the first firm had to pay a large penalty clause for failing to complete the task in time, as can be seen from the contemporary account books.

Ladies of the Post Office

The area outside the post office (built in 1882 and now a bank) was a favourite rendezvous for couples to meet up for dates, but inevitably there was sometimes the sad sight of a chap 'stood up' by his intended partner. The sense of irritation would sometimes be aggravated by local wags shouting out variants of 'Take one of them ladies out instead – they've got more life!' The 'ladies' they were referring to were statues on top of the post office of females representing Commerce, Steam, Electricity and Industry, and Genius and Science on either side of the Royal Crest. Across on the Town Hall, Commerce, Learning and Law are represented. For girls abandoned by their prospective boyfriends, male portrait busts of Cardinal Wolsey, King John and King Richard I decorate the Town Hall.

Lloyds Creepy Chambers

Lloyds Avenue is opposite the old post office on Cornhill. Originally there was just a narrow alleyway called Mumfords Passage which in 1931 got widened into a through road. Nowadays it has been made a pedestrians-only route. Lloyds Bank has some splendid carved columns containing tongue pokers and green men. The theme carries on inside the bank. Above the Lloyds Avenue archway are a group of offices known as Lloyds Chambers, accessed by stairs from Lloyds Avenue itself. They are let out to a number of businesses, from lawyers and accountants through to charities and publishers.

A single mum once told me her experience of working there. She was keen to get back to work when her daughter started school, and found another lady with a similar predicament: dropping her daughter off and collecting her, whilst working in

Town Hall and old post office.

Lloyds Avenue.

Green Man carving, Lloyds Bank.

between times. She approached an employment agency and found a part-time job with flexible hours in one of the many offices rented to a variety of small businesses in the building. She was required to do filing and copy typing from her bosses' pencil scrawled draft letters. He was quite happy that she started and finished early, so long as the work was done. It meant that her friend could drop the two girls off to school in the morning, and that she could collect them in the afternoon. She would arrive early each morning at the office, before anyone else (bar the cleaner) was about, and get on with her work, satisfied that her daughter was being looked after. One day her friend asked if it was possible to vary the arrangement for one day, as she needed to attend an early morning appointment. The boss at Lloyds Chambers agreed it was fine, so on the day in question she dropped the girls off to school and came into work a bit later. A cleaner was working at the top of the stairs, but not the familiar one who she had sometimes wished good morning. 'Where is your workmate this morning?' she asked. 'Is she alright?' The cleaner was puzzled. 'I haven't got a workmate,' she replied. 'I am the only cleaner working here.' The office worker described the woman she sometimes saw and called 'good morning' to at the end of the corridor, cleaning on her knees. The cleaner in front of her turned pale. 'That is the woman I replaced,' she gasped. 'She walked out onto Lloyds Avenue one morning after work and got run over and killed. I knew her slightly, and ended up working here in her place.'

The office worker never saw the quiet cleaner from the grave again, and left the job a few months later.

SELECT BIBLIOGRAPHY

Jennings, P., *Haunted Suffolk* (Tempus: Stroud, 2006)
Jennings, P., *Mysterious Ipswich* (Gruff: Ipswich, 2003)
Jennings, P., *Supernatural Ipswich* (Gruff: Ipswich, 1997)
Puttick, B., *Ghosts of Suffolk* (Countryside: Newbury, 1998)
Twinch, C., *Street by Street: Ipswich* (Breedon: Derby, 2006)

Further information on Original Gemini Ipswich Ghost Tours is available from www.geminighosts.co.uk or telephone 01473 462721.